DATA, DATA EVERYWHERE:

BRINGING ALL THE

DATA TOGETHER FOR

CONTINUOUS

SCHOOL IMPROVEMENT

VICTORIA L. BERNHARDT, Ph.D.
Executive Director
Education for the Future Initiative

Professor
Department of Professional Studies in Education
College of Communication and Education
California State University, Chico, CA

EYE ON EDUCATION
6 Depot Way West
Larchmont, NY 10538
(914) 833-0551
(914) 833-0761 Fax
www.eyeoneducation.com

For information about permission to reproduce selections from this book, write:
EYE ON EDUCATION
Permission Dept.
6 Depot Way West
Larchmont, NY 10538

Library of Congress Cataloging–in–Publication Data

Bernhardt, Victoria L., 1952-
    Data, data everywhere: Bringing all the data together for
continuous school improvement / by Victoria L. Bernhardt.
        p. cm.
    ISBN 978-1-59667-102-7
    1. School improvement programs—California—Livermore—
Data processing. 2. Marylin Avenue Elementary School
(Livermore, Calif.)—Data processing. I. Title.
LB2822.82.B467 2008
371.2'07—dc22
                                    2008043903

10 9 8 7 6 5 4 3 2 1

PREFACE

For years, people have been telling me that they appreciate the work of *Education for the Future,* and that it reflects what schools should be doing to improve teaching and learning for all students. However, some also ask—can you just give us a little data book that gets us started incorporating data into our work to get student achievement increases across the board?

So, here it is—a little data analysis book that contains *Victoria's Data Secrets*—the bare essentials for using data to improve teaching and learning. The activities described can be used with any level of educational organization—elementary, middle, high schools, districts, as well as special programs. Enjoy!

Sincerely,

Victoria L. Bernhardt, Ph.D.

Executive Director

Education for the Future Initiative

400 West First Street, Chico, CA 95929-0230

Tel: 530-898-4482 — Fax: 530-898-4484

e-mail: vbernhardt@csuchico.edu

website: *http://eff.csuchico.edu*

ACKNOWLEDGEMENTS

A huge thank you to Marylin Avenue staff for allowing us to learn from them. Their commitment to improvement is awesome. Their results are spectacular. Their willingness to share is greatly appreciated. A special thank you to Principal Jeff Keller and Leadership Team Leader Marfel Kusko for their perseverance with the change process, for reviewing article and book drafts, and for sharing their successes so others can learn.

I continue to be surrounded by such wonderful, helpful, and supportive people. The *Education for the Future* staff, Lynn Varicelli, Patsy Schutz, Brad Geise, Sally Withuhn, and Augie Fash, is always there to lend a helping hand with my publications, as well as every-day work. Lynn, once again, provided a beautiful layout. MC^2 did a great job on the cover. Patsy, Mike Derman, Robert Geise, Karen Raney, and Joy Rose were invaluable in providing concrete feedback to make the book more readable and helpful to readers. The feedback gave me the courage to keep going. Thank you all.

Sincerely,

Vickie Bernhardt

October 2008

ABOUT THE AUTHOR

Victoria L. Bernhardt, Ph.D., is Executive Director of the *Education for the Future Initiative,* a not-for-profit organization whose mission is to build the capacity of all learning organizations to gather, analyze, and use data to continuously improve learning for all students. She is also a Professor (currently on leave) in the Department of Professional Studies in Education, College of Communication and Education, at California State University, Chico. Dr. Bernhardt is the author of the following books, all published by Eye on Education, Larchmont, New York:

- ▼ *Translating Data into Information to Improve Teaching and Learning* (2007).

- ▼ A four-book (with CD-Roms) collection of using data to improve student learning—*Using Data to Improve Student Learning in Elementary Schools* (2003); *Using Data to Improve Student Learning in Middle Schools* (2004); *Using Data to Improve Student Learning in High Schools* (2005); and *Using Data to Improve Student Learning in School Districts* (2006).

- ▼ *Data Analysis for Continuous School Improvement* (First Edition, 1998; Second Edition, 2004).

▼ *The School Portfolio Toolkit: A Planning, Implementation, and Evaluation Guide for Continuous School Improvement,* with CD-Rom (2002).

▼ *The Example School Portfolio* (2000).

▼ *The School Portfolio: A Comprehensive Framework for School Improvement* (First Edition, 1994; Second Edition, 1999).

▼ Currently in press: *Questionnaires Demystified: Using Perceptions Data for Continuous Improvement.* Co-authored with Bradley J. Geise.

Available about the time this book is published: Check the *Education for the Future* website (*http://eff.csuchico.edu*) for the link to our automated *SchoolPortfolio* tool.

Dr. Bernhardt is passionate about her mission of helping all educators continuously improve student learning in their classrooms, their schools, their districts, states, and provinces by gathering, analyzing, and using actual data—as opposed to using hunches and "gut-level" feelings. She has made numerous presentations at professional meetings and conducts workshops and Institutes on the school portfolio, data analysis, process measurement, and school improvement at local, state, regional, national, and international levels.

Dr. Bernhardt can be reached at:

Victoria L. Bernhardt, Ph.D.
Executive Director
Education for the Future Initiative
400 West First Street, Chico, CA 95929-0230
Tel: 530-898-4482 — Fax: 530-898-4484
e-mail: vbernhardt@csuchico.edu
website: *http://eff.csuchico.edu*

CONTENTS

1

INTRODUCTION

In July 2006, seven members of the Marylin Avenue Elementary School (Livermore, California) Leadership Team arrived at the annual *Education for the Future* Summer Data Institute in Chico, California, ready and eager to learn how to use data to improve instruction and student learning. Members of the team included six teachers, the district data analyst, and Principal Jeff, who just finished his first year as a school administrator.

All team members were eager to learn, although they were distraught about what to do regarding their situation:

▼ Their school had not made Adequate Yearly Progress (AYP) since 2004

▼ They just found out they were in "Program Improvement"

▼ Their English as a Second Language population kept increasing

▼ Their free/reduced lunch population kept increasing

▼ It was perceived that the school culture was not ready to change

▼ The school lacked focus and instructional coherence

▼ Staff was not using data to improve

After a week of intensive work, the team left with a plan for the data-driven activities to implement to improve instruction and student learning.

One year later, on July 25, 2007, three members of the Marylin Avenue Elementary School Leadership Team returned to Chico for the 2007 *Education for the Future* Summer Data Institute. Their mission was very different from the previous year—this time, they came to share their successes.

Just days before they arrived in Chico, the school received its Spring 2007 student achievement results—the school's student achievement results improved at *every grade level, in every subject area but one at one grade level, and with all student groups.* These increases came even as the Hispanic and free/reduced lunch populations increased even more than the previous years.

This book relates what Marylin Avenue School teachers and administrators did to improve teaching and learning between the last week in July 2006 and the end of the 2006-07 school year to get those increases, and what every school needs to know about data analysis to get student achievement increases at every grade level, in every subject area, and with every subgroup, in one year, and then keep it going.

MARYLIN AVENUE DEMOGRAPHICS

In 2002-03, 49% of Marylin Avenue's students were of Hispanic descent; this percentage increased to 66% five years later as the percentage of Caucasian students decreased from 31% to 18%. At the same time, the percentage of students receiving free/reduced lunch increased from more than 45% to almost 76% of the population. By 2006-07, Marilyn Avenue School had a student enrollment of 507 in grades K through 5, up from 465 in 2002-03. Of the 507 students enrolled, 335 (66%) spoke Spanish as their first language. Almost half of the parents had only a high school diploma or less. The teaching staff, mostly Caucasian females, had an average of 14.4 years of teaching experience.

Figure 1.1
Marylin Avenue Elementary School Background

Student Enrollment	2002-03		2006-07	
Total	465		507	
Hispanic	229	49.2%	335	66.1%
Caucasian	145	31.2%	91	17.9%
Other	91	19.6%	81	16.0%
Free/Reduced Lunch Qualifiers	211	45.4%	385	75.8%
Mobility	30%		34%	

Marylin Avenue had not made AYP for the previous four years. The California Academic Performance Index (API)[1] showed the school getting negative numbers for the previous three years, which basically meant that student achievement results were decreasing across the board. In 2003-04, the school went backward 17 API points. Their target for 2006-07 was to increase 7 API points.

Figure 1.2
Marylin Avenue Elementary School
API Growth and Targets Met, 2002-03 to 2005-06

Year	Number Tested	Base	Target	Actual	Met Target
2002-03	276	681	6	1	No
2003-04	270	665	6	-17	No
2004-05	313	662	7	-5	No
2005-06	303	651	7	-7	No

---

[1]*California Academic Performance Index (API):* Introduced in California in 1999, the API measures the academic performance and progress of individual schools and establishes growth targets for future academic improvement. It is a numeric index (or scale) that ranges from a low of 200 to a high of 1000. A school's score or placement on the API is an indicator of a school's performance level. The interim statewide API performance target for all schools is 800. A school's growth is measured by how well it is moving toward or past that goal.

The Leadership Team felt the biggest challenge was to get experienced teachers to realize that changes in the population required changes in their approaches to teaching.

July 2007

Fast forward to the 2007 Summer Data Institute. The message Principal Jeff and the team enthusiastically shared with Institute participants was about how the school increased 54 API points and got student achievement increases in every grade level, every subject area, and with every student group. Here is the message relayed to the group assembled in Chico—

▼ *We looked at all the school's data*—comprehensive demographic data gave us the context of how our current student population was changing, which told us we had to change our strategies and services or we would never get all students proficient; perceptions data allowed us to hear from the students and parents about how better to meet their needs; perceptions data from staff revealed what it would take to change teaching strategies and get all staff working "on the same page"; student learning results, disaggregated in all ways, told us where we did not have instructional coherence and which students we were not reaching. We realized we had very little school processes data that measured our instructional strategies and programs. Looking at all the data gave us a reality check about where our school was, not just where we thought it was.

▼ *We used the Education for the Future Continuous Improvement Continuums* (CICs) to help the staff see what everyone was thinking regarding where the school was with respect to a continuous improvement framework. This helped us get all staff on the same page so we could move forward together.

▼ *We developed a vision.* All the data and the results of the CICs told us we needed a clear vision for the school that everyone could commit to, not just agree with, and one that we would monitor to make sure everyone was implementing in the manner intended. Having a vision that was shared by everyone made a huge difference.

▼ *All staff participated in identifying contributing causes of our undesirable results.* Using the *Education for the Future* problem-solving cycle activity helped staff engage in deep discussions and honestly think about an issue before solving it. In the past, we would identify a gap and then solve it in the same half hour. The problem-solving cycle made us think through an issue and gather data to understand it in greater depth before solving it. Staff used this activity for evaluating programs, strategies, and processes.

▼ *We engaged in schoolwide professional learning in assessment and instructional strategies.* We wanted teachers to work differently, so we had to support their continual learning of new assessment and instructional strategies.

▼ *We began using common assessments to clarify where students were at any time during the year.*

▼ *We established collaborative teams, and meeting times were enforced.* Teams used the time to discuss student assessment results and student work and how to change instructional strategies to get improved results. We kept these times sacred and modeled how to use the time and data effectively. We shifted our focus from teaching to learning.

▼ As a part of our follow-up to the 2006 Summer Institute, *we began the creation of a School Portfolio to house our data, vision, and plan.* The School Portfolio helps us assess where we are at any time with respect to our vision. The Portfolio provides the focus and sense of urgency to improve.

LAYOUT OF THIS BOOK

The purpose of *Data, Data Everywhere* is to describe how you can use data to get student achievement increases at every grade level, every subject area, and with every student group—in one year and then maintain it. Using the Marylin Avenue story as the impetus, the chapters flow as follows:

Chapter 2 is about *Looking at all the School's Data.* The chapter outlines what data are important for across the board increases, and how these data make the difference.

Chapter 3 describes the self-assessment tools that Marylin Avenue used, tools that you can also use to determine where staff thinks the school is, and what your school needs to do to improve.

Chapter 4 explains why a vision is the most important piece of information your staff can share, and provide a process for getting a shared vision.

Chapter 5 shows how you can quickly, easily, and in a fun way get to contributing causes of any school problem.

Chapter 6 focuses on the strategies to implement a school vision that will help you achieve student achievement increases across the board.

Chapter 7 shows how the data work together with a vision to create a continuous improvement plan that gets implemented.

Chapter 8 concludes this book with overall recommendations to schools for getting student achievement increases at every grade level, subject area, and student group in one year, and provides advice to professional learning coordinators and to district administrators on how to lead this work at the district level.

Appendices: Appendix A contains the *Education for the Future Continuous Improvement Continuums* for schools and districts. Appendix B contains a staff-developed *Vision Rubric Example* for monitoring the implemention of the school vision.

2

LOOKING AT ALL
THE SCHOOL'S DATA

We looked at all the school's data—comprehensive demographic data gave us the context of how our population was changing, which told us we had to change our strategies and services or we would never get all students proficient; perceptions data allowed us to hear from the students and parents about how better to meet their needs; perceptions data from staff revealed what it would take to change teaching strategies and get all staff working "on the same page"; student learning results, disaggregated in all ways, told us where we did not have instructional coherence and which students we were not reaching. We realized we had very little school processes data—the data that measure our instructional processes and programs. Looking at all the data gave us a reality check about where our school was, not just where we thought it was.

Marylin Avenue School

Many educators believe that more than 50 percent of student achievement results can be explained by *other factors* than what goes on in school. With educators believing this, if we want to change the results we are getting, we have to understand why we are getting the results we are getting. Then we need to change what we do in order to get different results.

To understand the whole experience of school, we need to gather data in more than one area. Multiple measures of data include *four* major types of data—not just student learning, but also demographics, perceptions, and school processes. Analyses of *demographics, perceptions, student learning,* and *school processes* provide a powerful picture that helps us understand the school's impact on student achievement. When used together, these measures give schools the information they need to improve teaching and learning. In Figure 2.1, the four multiple measures of data are shown as overlapping circles. Commonly called "the four circles," the figure illustrates the types of information that one can capture from individual measures and the enhanced levels of analyses that can be gained from the intersections of the measures. One measure by itself gives useful information. Comprehensive measures, used together and over time, provide much richer information. Ultimately, schools need to be able to predict what they must do to meet the needs of *all* students they have, or will have in the future. The information gleaned from the intersections of these four measures (demographics, perceptions, student learning, and school processes) helps us to define the questions we want to ask, and focuses us on what data are necessary in order to find the answers.

Demographic data provide descriptive information about the school community, such as student enrollment, attendance, grade level, ethnicity, gender, native language, staff gender, ethnicity, years of teaching, and credential status. Demographic data are very important for us to understand. They are the part of our educational system over which we have little or no control, but with which we can observe trends and glean information for purposes of prediction and

Figure 2.1
Multiple Measures of Data

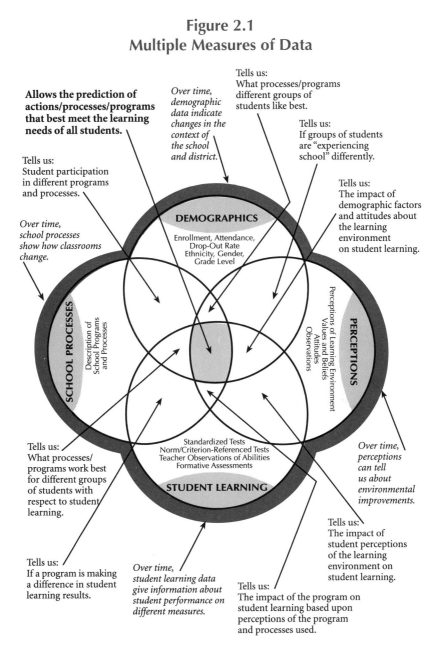

Tells us:
What processes/programs
different groups of
students like best.

**Allows the prediction of
actions/processes/programs
that best meet the learning
needs of all students.**

*Over time,
demographic
data indicate
changes in the
context of
the school
and district.*

Tells us:
If groups of students
are "experiencing
school" differently.

Tells us:
Student participation
in different programs
and processes.

*Over time,
school processes
show how classrooms
change.*

Tells us:
The impact of
demographic factors
and attitudes about
the learning
environment
on student learning.

DEMOGRAPHICS

Enrollment, Attendance,
Drop-Out Rate
Ethnicity, Gender,
Grade Level

SCHOOL PROCESSES

Description of
School Programs
and Processes

Perceptions of Learning Environment
Values and Beliefs
Attitudes
Observations

PERCEPTIONS

Standardized Tests
Norm/Criterion-Referenced Tests
Teacher Observations of Abilities
Formative Assessments

STUDENT LEARNING

Tells us:
What processes/
programs work best
for different groups
of students with
respect to student
learning.

*Over time,
perceptions
can tell
us about
environmental
improvements.*

Tells us:
The impact of
student perceptions
of the learning
environment on
student learning.

Tells us:
If a program is making
a difference in student
learning results.

*Over time,
student learning data
give information about
student performance on
different measures.*

Tells us:
The impact of the program on
student learning based upon
perceptions of the program
and processes used.

planning. Demographic data assist us in understanding all parts of our educational system through the disaggregation of other measures by demographic variables.

Perceptions data help us understand what students, parents, teachers, and others think about the learning environment. Perceptions can be gathered in a variety of ways—through questionnaires, interviews, and observations. Perceptions are important since people act in congruence with what they believe, perceive, or think about different topics. It is important to know student, teacher, and parent perceptions of the school so school personnel know what they need to do to improve the system. Perceptions data can also tell us what is possible with respect to change.

Student Learning describes the results of our educational system in terms of standardized test results, grades, standards assessments, and formative assessments. Student learning can help us know what students are learning, what teachers are teaching, and which students need extra help. Schools use a variety of student learning measurements—usually separately—and sometimes without thinking about how these measurements are interrelated. Schools normally think of multiple measures as looking only at different measures of student learning, rather than including demographics, perceptions, and school processes.

School Processes define what educators are doing to get the results that they are getting, and how they work. School Processes include curriculum, instructional strategies, processes, and programs. Special education, bilingual education, gifted, and advanced placement are examples of common programs. Project-based learning, differentiated instruction, and formative assessments are examples of processes used in classrooms. This is the category of data that seems to be the hardest to measure, but it is the area in which educators have the most control. To change the results schools are getting, teachers and school personnel must begin to document these processes and align them with the results in order to understand what to change to get different results, and to share their successes with others.

A SNAPSHOT OF THE MEASURES

Looking at each of the four measures separately, we get snapshots of data in isolation from any other data at the school level. At this level we can answer questions such as—

▼ How many students are enrolled in the school this year? *(Demographic)*

▼ How satisfied are parents, students, and/or staff with the learning environment? *(Perceptions)*

▼ How did students at the school score on a test? *(Student Learning)*

▼ What programs are operating in the school this year? *(School Processes)*

By looking over time we can answer questions such as, but not limited to:

▼ How has enrollment in the school changed over the past five years? *(Demographics)*

▼ How have student perceptions of the learning environment changed over time? *(Perceptions)*

▼ Are there differences in student scores on standardized tests over the years? *(Student Learning)*

▼ What programs have operated in the school in the past five years? *(School Processes)*

Intersection of Two Measures

Crossing two measures, we begin to see a more vivid picture of the school, allowing us to answer questions such as:

▼ Do students who attend school every day perform better on state assessments than students who miss more than five days per month? *(Demographics by Student Learning)*

▼ What strategies do third-grade teachers use with students whose native languages are different from that of the teacher? *(Demographics by School Processes)*

▼ Is there a gender difference in students' perceptions of the learning environment? *(Demographics by Perceptions)*

▼ Do students with positive attitudes about school do better academically, as measured by state assessments? *(Perceptions by Student Learning)*

▼ Are there differences in how students enrolled in different programs perceive the learning environment? *(School Processes by Perceptions)*

▼ Do students who were enrolled in active, hands-on content courses perform better on standardized achievement tests than those who took the content courses in a more traditional manner? *(School Processes by Student Learning)*

Looking at the interaction of two of the measures over time allows us to see trends as they develop (e.g., standardized achievement scores disaggregated by ethnicity over the past three years can help us see if the equality of scores, by ethnicity, is truly a trend or an initial fluctuation).

Intersection of Three Measures

As we intersect three of the measures at the school level (e.g., student learning disaggregated by ethnicity compared to student questionnaire responses disaggregated by ethnicity), the types of questions that we are able to answer include the following:

▼ Do students of different ethnicities perceive the learning environment differently, and are their scores on standardized achievement tests consistent with these perceptions? *(Demographics by Perceptions by Student Learning)*

▼ What instructional process(es) did the previously non-English-speaking students enjoy most in their all-English classrooms this year? *(Perceptions by Demographics by School Processes)*

▼ Is there a difference in students' reports of what they like most about the school by whether or not they participate in extracurricular activities? Do these students have higher grades than students who do not participate in extracurricular activities? *(Perceptions by Student Learning by School Processes)*

▼ Which program is making the biggest difference with respect to student achievement for at-risk students this year, and is one group of students responding "better" to the processes? *(School Processes by Student Learning by Demographics)*

Looking at three measures over time allows us to see trends, to begin to understand the learning environment from the students' perspectives, and to know how to deliver instruction to get the desired results from and for all students.

Intersection of Four Measures

Our ultimate analysis is the intersection of all four measures, at the school level (e.g., standardized achievement tests disaggregated by program, by gender, by grade level, compared to questionnaire results for students by program, by gender, by grade level). These interactions allow us to answer a question such as:

▼ Are there differences in achievement scores for eighth-grade girls and boys who report that they like school, by the type of program and grade level in which they are enrolled? *(Demographics by Perceptions by School Processes by Student Learning)*

It is not until we intersect all four circles, at the school level, and over time, that we are able to answer questions that will predict if the actions, processes, and programs that we establish will meet the needs of all students. With this intersection, we can answer the ultimate question:

▼ Based on whom we have as students, how they prefer to learn, and what programs they are in, are all students learning at the same rate? *(Student Learning by Demographics by Perceptions by School Processes)*

LOOKING AT ALL THE DATA

Looking at all the data means building a data profile to see where a school is on all four data types. The four circles quickly tell the story of your school. The good news is—if you do not like the story of your school, you can change it. You just have to know where the school honestly is at this point in time. We often try to change schools from where we think they are, instead of from where they actually are. This is why some schools with seemingly sound plans do not make progress.

Principal Jeff described looking at multiple measures as one of the most enlightened lessons for staff. Marylin Avenue found that as the student population changed over time, the teachers stayed basically the same. This caused them to think that maybe new professional learning was required to understand how to meet the needs of the students they have now and will have in the future. Their perceptions results led them to develop a behavior plan, to improve yard duty supervision, and to improve staff communication. Student learning data showed staff members they needed to know more about student performance along the way in order to adjust processes. School process analyses helped them improve attendance, and effectively utilize interventions and data teams. Looking at all the data together allowed them to achieve instructional coherence—they understood which processes worked for which students and how to achieve results across grade levels, and over time.

SUMMARY

The moral of the story is—if we want to get different results, we have to change the processes that create the results. Just looking at summative student learning measures, only, focuses teachers on the results; it does not give them information about what they need to do to get different results. Just looking at student learning measures could, in fact, keep teachers from progressing and truly meeting the needs of students. When schools focus only on student learning measures, we see school personnel using their time to figure out how to fix the students who are not achieving. We want school personnel to use their time to figure out how to provide a better learning experience for all students. Looking at all four types of data over time provides an excellent beginning for determining how to improve learning for *all* students.

3

SELF ASSESSMENT

We used the Education for the Future Continuous Improvement Continuums to help the staff see what everyone was thinking regarding where the school was with respect to a continuous improvement framework. This helped us get all staff on the same page so we could move forward together.

Marylin Avenue School

The *Education for the Future Continuous Improvement Continuums* (CICs) are self-assessment tools that measure, on a one-to-five scale, where the school is with respect to its *approach, implementation,* and *outcome* for seven continuous improvement categories. Adapted from the *Malcolm Baldrige National Award Program for Quality Business Management,* the continuums provide an authentic means for measuring systemic improvement and growth. (See Appendix A for the *School and District Continuous Improvement Continuums.*) Schools use these continuums as a vehicle for ongoing self-assessment. They use the results of the assessment to find out—

▼ where they really are, as a staff;

▼ to acknowledge their accomplishments;

▼ to get all staff on the same page;

▼ to set goals for improvement; and

▼ to keep school districts and partners apprised of the progress they have made in their school improvement efforts.

The seven *Continuous Improvement Continuums* comprise the categories below:

1. *Information and Analysis* is a critical element in planning for change, and in supporting continual school improvement. Schools must analyze existing data and collect additional information to understand how to meet the needs of their clients, to understand the contributing causes of problems or undesirable results, to assess growth, and to predict the types of educational programs that will be needed in the future. The intent of this continuum is to establish systematic and rigorous reliance on data for decision making in all parts of the organization.

2. *Student Achievement* describes strategies for increasing student achievement—the school's "Constancy of Purpose."

The intent of this component is to support schools in moving from a fire-fighting approach, to one of systemic *prevention* of student failure; from teachers who provide information, to facilitators who understand and can predict the impact of their actions on student achievement; and students from recipients of knowledge delivery, to goal-setting self-assessors who produce independent, quality work.

3. *Quality Planning* by schools must be strategic or change efforts will not be implemented. A well-defined and well-executed school improvement effort is based on a strategic plan that provides a logical direction for change and lays out the action to the vision. This continuum assists schools in developing the elements of a strategic plan, including:

   ▼ a *mission* that describes the purpose of the school;

   ▼ a *vision* that represents how the school will carry out its mission;

   ▼ *goals* that promote the mission and vision; an *action plan*—procedural steps needed to implement the goals, including timelines and accountability;

   ▼ *outcome measures;* and

   ▼ a *plan* for continuous improvement and evaluation.

4. *Professional Learning* helps staff members, teachers, and principals change the manner in which they work—

   ▼ how they collaborate and make decisions;

   ▼ how they gather, analyze, and utilize data;

   ▼ how they plan, teach, and monitor achievement; and

   ▼ how they evaluate personnel and assess the impact of new approaches to instruction and assessment on students.

Professional learning provides individuals with opportunities to improve their personal performance on a continuous basis and to learn new skills for working with each other in reforming their culture and workplace.

5. *Leadership* focuses on creating a learning environment that encourages everyone to contribute to making school have a cumulative, purposeful effect on all student learning. A quality leadership infrastructure emphasizes the prevention of problems—such as student failure—as opposed to short-term solving or covering up of problems, and makes the school change effort conceivable. This continuum assists schools in thinking through shared decision making and leadership structures that will work with their specific population, climate, and vision. The Leadership Continuum calls for leaders who understand that their job is to help everyone in the organization implement the vision.

6. *Partnership Development* with the school's community must benefit all partners. This continuum assists schools in understanding the purposes of, approaches to, and planning for educational partnerships with business and community groups, parents, other educational professionals, and students.

7. *Continuous Improvement and Evaluation* of all operations of the school is essential to schools seeking improvement in the manner in which they do business. This continuum assists schools in further understanding the interrelationships of the components of continuous improvement and in improving their processes and products.

UNDERSTANDING THE CONTINUUMS

These continuums, evaluated on the one to five scale horizontally, represent a range of criteria related to continuous improvement with respect to an *Approach* to the Continuum, *Implementation* of the approach, and the *Outcome* that results from the implementation. (Figure 3.1 shows the Information and Analysis Continuum. The complete set of continuums appear in Appendix A.) A *one* rating, located at the left of each continuum, represents a school that has not yet begun to improve. *Five*, located at the right of each continuum, represents a school that is one step removed from "world class quality." The elements between one and five describe how that continuum is hypothesized to evolve in a continuously improving school. Each continuum moves from a reactive mode to a proactive mode—from fire fighting to prevention. The score of *five* in *approach*, *implementation*, and *outcome* in each continuum is the target.

Vertically, the *Approach, Implementation,* and *Outcome* statements, for any number one through five, are hypotheses. In other words, the implementation statement describes how the approach might look when implemented, and the outcome is the "pay-off" for implementing the approach. If the hypotheses are accurate, the outcome will not be realized until the approach is actually implemented.

Figure 3.1 A
School Continuous Improvement Continuum
INFORMATION AND ANALYSIS

	One	Two	Three
Approach	Data or information about student performance and needs are not gathered in any systematic way; there is no way to determine what needs to change at the school, or classroom levels, based on data.	There is no systematic process, but some teacher and student information is collected and used to problem solve.	School collects data related to student performance (e.g., attendance, enrollment, achievement) and conducts surveys on student, teacher, and parent needs. The information is used to drive the strategic quality plan for school change.
Implementation	No information is gathered with which to make changes. Student dissatisfaction with the learning process is seen as an irritation, not a need for improvement.	Some data are tracked, such as attendance, drop-out rates, and enrollment. Only a few individuals are asked for feedback about areas of schooling.	School collects information on current and former students (e.g., demographics, student learning, and perceptions), analyzes and uses it in conjunction with future trends for planning.
Outcome	Only anecdotal and hypothetical information are available about student performance, behavior, and perceptions. Problems are solved individually with short-term results.	Little data are available. Change is limited to some areas of the school depending upon individual teachers and their efforts.	Information collected about student and parent needs, assessment, and instructional practices is shared with the school staff and used to plan for change. Information helps staff understand pressing issues, and track results for improvement.

Figure 3.1 B
School Continuous Improvement Continuum
INFORMATION AND ANALYSIS

Four	Five	
There is systematic and systemic reliance on data (including data for all student groups) as a basis for decision making at the classroom level as well as at the school level. Changes are based on the study of data to meet the needs of students and teachers.	Information is gathered in all areas of student interaction with the school throughout the school year. Teachers engage students in gathering information on their own performance. Accessible to all levels, data are comprehensive in scope and an accurate reflection of school quality.	Approach
Data, including school processes, are used to improve the effectiveness of teaching strategies on all student learning. Students' historical performances are graphed and utilized for diagnostics. Student evaluations and performances are analyzed and used by teachers in all classrooms to continually improve instruction. Contributing causes are analyzed.	Innovative teaching processes that meet the needs of students are implemented to the delight of teachers, parents, and students. Information is analyzed and used to prevent student failure, and to evaluate all processes and programs. Contributing causes are known through analyses. Problems are prevented through the use of data.	Implementation
A data system is in place. Positive trends begin to appear in most classrooms and schoolwide. There is evidence that these results are caused by understanding and effectively using data, including analyzing for contributing causes.	Students are delighted with the school's instructional processes and proud of their own capabilities to learn and assess their own growth. Good to excellent achievement is the result for all students. No student falls through the cracks. Teachers use data to predict and prevent potential problems. Schoolwide, only "effective" processes and programs are used.	Outcome

Using the Continuums

Schools use the *Continuous Improvement Continuums* to understand where they are with respect to continuous improvement. The results help get *all* staff on the same page with respect to what needs to change and provide that sense of urgency needed to spark enthusiasm for school improvement efforts.

The most beneficial approach to assessing on the continuums is to gather the entire staff together for the assessment. Each staff member should be given a copy of the continuums and a larger version should be posted on the wall (Appendix A). When assessing on the continuums for the first time, plan for three hours to complete all seven categories. Start the assessment by stating or creating the ground rules, setting the tone for a safe and confidential assessment, and explaining why you are doing this. Provide a brief overview of the seven sections.

The specific process for assessing on the continuums follows:

1. Establish ground rules for the assessment. We want to make sure everyone understands that the conversation is safe and confidential. Also clarify why it is important to do this activity.

2. Introduce the first section of the continuums— *Information and Analysis.* Ask staff members to read the *Information and Analysis Continuous Improvement Continuum* and see if they can recognize where the school is right now, with respect to *Approach, Implementation,* and *Outcome.* Start with a one and move to a five. Keep the group moving and try to avoid rewording the descriptions of the continuums.

3. Direct staff members to walk over to the *Information and Analysis Continuum* on the wall and place a colorful dot or flag where they believe the school is with respect to *Approach, Implementation,* and *Outcome.* We call this "dotmocracy." (See photo below.)

4. After everyone has placed her or his dot, review what you see. Focusing on *Approach,* ask for discussion of why staff thought the school was a 1, 2, 3, 4, or 5. Record highlights of the discussion.

Dotmocracy Photo

5. After the discussion, if one number is becoming clearly favored, ask if there is anyone who could not live with this number as a baseline assessment of this school's *Approach* to *Information and Analysis.* If no one opposes, write that number on a post it and place it on the large continuum to represent the consensus decision of the group. If there is not a number that is clearly favored after the first discussion, continue the discussion. You can assist if there is a stalemate by systematically asking what the organization has for *Information and Analysis,* and walking through each number in *Approach,* clarifying what the organization would have to have to be a specific number. Ask again for a show of hands.

6. Continue with *Implementation* and *Outcome.*

7. When consensus on the three sections is complete, ask for the "Next Steps." What do we need to do to move up? Or to become the next solid number?

8. Continue with the next six continuums. After *Information and Analysis,* you can usually introduce two continuums at a time. (If you are familiar with the continuums, you could read and dot two or three at the same time. You will need to discuss each one separately to list "next steps.")

9. As staff is reading the next continuum, use the time to type highlights of the discussion on the just completed continuum. You will be able to leave with a complete report that summarizes the assessment results that day.

10. Add digital pictures of the assessment charts to the report to watch the staff thinking come together over time.

We want the *Continuous Improvement Continuums* to add a sense of urgency for improvement. To that end, do not let staff members average their scores or rate themselves too high. Make sure they think about, and write, next steps.

Averaging the scores does not inspire change—especially on the first assessment. If the discussion hangs between two numbers, go to the lower number, and write solid next steps to become the next number.

Make sure everyone knows the emphasis is on consensus and not a vote. We want everyone to win!

Periodic (regular) assessment sessions will help staffs see that they are making progress. The decision of how often to assess on the *Continuous Improvement Continuums* is certainly up to the school. We recommend at least once a year—about mid-fall or mid-spring—when there is time in the current school year to implement next steps. Some schools use them in both the fall and spring every year. Most use them twice the first year and then once during each of the following years. Using these continuums will enable you and your school to stay motivated and to keep everyone on the same page with continuous improvement, to shape and maintain your shared vision. Take photos of the resulting charts. Even if your consensus number does not increase, the dots will most probably come together over time showing shifts in whole staff thinking (as with the example in Figure 3.2, which shows how the staff moved away from a two-three level to a strong three). Continuous improvement is a never-ending process which, when used effectively, will ultimately lead your school toward providing a *quality educational experience for all children* and positive teaching experiences for all staff members.

Figure 3.2
Continuum Assessment Progress Over Time

Fall Assessment

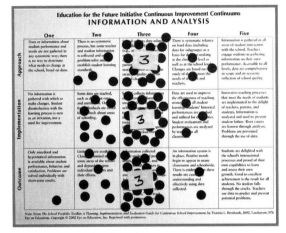

Spring Assessment

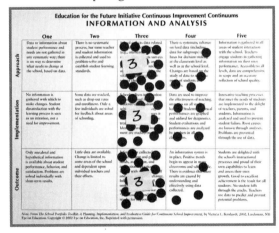

Assessing with the Education for the Future Continuous Improvement Continuums

Marylin Avenue staff members assessed their school using the *Education for the Future Continuous Improvement Continuums*. They came to consensus on a baseline assessment. The results told them they needed to:

▼ gather, analyze, and use all types of data effectively to understand where they are now, how they got there, and what they need to do to get different results.

▼ adopt common formative assessments that reflect the standards and predict the high-stakes assessments.

▼ learn to use all assessments effectively.

▼ create a vision that is clear, shared, and committed to by the entire staff.

▼ create a shared decision-making structure that helps everyone use data and implement the vision.

▼ create a plan to implement the vision, based on the data

▼ monitor the vision to support all staff in implementing the vision.

▼ engage in schoolwide professional learning in using "power" standards in the classroom, using common formative assessments, differentiating instruction, and effectively teaching students of poverty and those with English as a second language.

▼ get all teachers collaborating on improving student learning through common formative assessments and targeting instruction.

 ▼ create a plan for including parents and the
   community in helping them reach their vision.
 ▼ evaluate all parts of the school on an ongoing basis.

SUMMARY

Assessing on the *Education for the Future Continuous Improvement Continuums* will help staffs see where their systems are right now with respect to continuous improvement, and ultimately show that they are making progress over time. The discussion that leads to consensus is the most valuable piece of this activity. In addition to helping the entire staff see where the school is, the discussion tells every staff member what each one needs to do to continuously improve.

4

THE VISION

We developed a vision. All the data and the results of the Continuous Improvement Continuums told us we needed a clear vision for the school that everyone could commit to, not just agree with, and one that we would monitor to make sure everyone was implementing in the manner intended. Having a vision that was shared by everyone made a huge difference.

Marylin Avenue School

True data-driven decision making is only partly about data. A clear, shared vision and leadership play major roles in data-driven decision making. If there is no focus or unified front in a school, there is also no continuum of learning that will make sense for students and no structure to get student achievement increases. Figure 4.1 shows that *Random Acts of Improvement* result when there is no target.

Strong leadership inspires a shared vision and ensures its implementation. A strong leader also encourages and models the analysis and use of data. A continuous improvement process can ensure that all professional development is focused on implementing the vision, that all staff members understand their roles in implementing the vision and helping students learn, and that there is continuous evaluation to know how to improve on an ongoing basis to reach school goals. The vision is the key to getting *Focused Acts of Improvement* (Figure 4.2).

Figure 4.1
Random Acts of Improvement

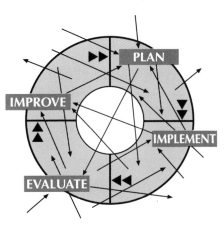

Figure 4.2
Focused Acts of Improvement

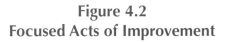
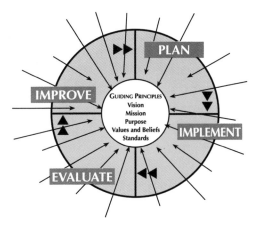

INSPIRING A SHARED VISION

To create a vision that is truly shared—committed to unanimously and understood in the same way—we must build on the values and beliefs of the school staff members to create core values and beliefs, a core purpose, and a mission for the school. With core values and beliefs, purpose and mission, a vision can be created for the school.

We must begin with the personal and move to the collective. Systems thinker, Peter Senge,[1] sums up the rationale:

> *Shared visions emerge from personal visions.*
> *This is how they derive their energy*
> *and how they foster commitment...*
> *If people don't have their own vision, all they*
> *can do is "sign up" for someone else's.*
> *The result is compliance, never commitment.*

Visions that get implemented are specific and clear, so everyone can understand them in the same way. That is what *shared* means. We like to see staff members' values and beliefs reflected in the curriculum, instruction, assessment, and environment. If staff members believe these things will impact learning for all students, they will do them, leading to a truly shared vision for the school that gets implemented.

ACTION PLAN

↑

SHARED VISION

↑

Mission

↑

PURPOSE

↑

Values and Beliefs

---

[1]Senge, Peter (2006). *The Fifth Discipline: The Art and Practice of the Learning Organization.* New York: NY: Doubleday Business.

PROCESS FOR CREATING A SHARED VISION

To create a shared vision, gather all staff members together in a location with tables that seat 5 to 7 people. Organize seating arrangements to ensure a mixture (grade level/subjects taught) in the small groups and to ensure that time will be used effectively.

Prior to the session, staff members should be well-versed in the literature about what works in schools like theirs. The steps that follow describe the process in detail.

1. **Review Ground Rules**

   ▼ This is a safe room

   ▼ There is no rank in this room

   ▼ All ideas are valid

   ▼ Each person gets a chance to speak

   ▼ Each person gets a chance to listen

   ▼ We are here to focus on the future

   ▼ Our purpose is improvement, not blame

2. **Determine Core Values and Beliefs**

   Have the members of the group *individually* brainstorm and document their thoughts about: *What are the curriculum, instruction, assessment, and environmental factors that support effective learning for our students?* (10 minutes, or longer if needed)

   Compare and merge ideas in *small groups.* Write the ideas on poster paper. It is okay to add or to agree to ideas that were not on an individual's original list. Stick to the topic. (15-20 minutes)

   Reconvene as a *large group.* Someone from each group stands next to the group's posters to note duplicates and to report. Start on one end of the room, for example, and have the reporter for the first group read all of the group's ideas about curriculum. Other groups note duplications on their poster and when it is their turn, report what they have left. Start with a different group for each category and vary the direction so each group gets maximum exposure.

Come to agreement on core values and beliefs for the school. *Recorder types on a laptop so statements are displayed on the screen.* (30 minutes) (There is no limit to the number of core values and beliefs. However, after this day, with staff approval, the Leadership Team might merge some ideas if the list is very long and overlapping.)

3. **Determine the Core Purpose**

Have staff members *individually* brainstorm and document personal ideas about the purpose of the school—*do not worry about the wording at this point.* (5 minutes)

Share individual purposes in *small groups* and post a common purpose with which everyone in the small group can live. (10 minutes)

Look for commonalities across the small group purposes with the *large group.* Come to agreement on a core purpose for the school. *Recorder types the core purpose on the laptop.* (15-20 minutes)

Print the core values and beliefs and purpose for each participant to use for the next step.

4. **Revisit the Mission**

Review the current mission statement. Either agree that the current mission is fine, or that a committee will craft the mission statement at a different time using the core values and beliefs and purpose, and bring it back to the whole staff. As long as the purpose is clear, the process can proceed without the mission statement being completely written.

It is the purpose that is most important. Determine who will write the mission. *Use the existing mission, update it quickly, or delegate the mission to be rewritten. Move on.* (5-10 minutes)

5. **Create a Vision**

Still assembled in the large group, *individuals* brainstorm and document personal visions for the school in terms of what the school would *look like, sound like, feel like* if we were doing what we need to do for our children—if we were living our core values and beliefs, purpose, and mission. Identify curriculum, instruction, assessment, and environmental components. (*Note:* If the core values and beliefs are done well, the individuals will say "The vision should be our core values and beliefs," which is what we would like to see happen.) (10 minutes)

Share personal visions in *small groups* and document commonalities. It is okay to add or to agree to ideas that were not on an individual's original list. Post ideas. (15 minutes—sometimes this step can be skipped if the note about values and beliefs holds true.)

Come to agreement on the commonalities with the *large group.* Come to agreement on the elements of the vision for the school. *Make sure everyone understands that these agreements become commitments for implementation.* (30 minutes)

6. **Determine School Goals—The Outcomes of the Vision**

There should be only two or three school goals. Again, have *individuals* take time to do their own thinking. (5 minutes)

Share individual ideas in *small groups* and document commonalities. (10 minutes)

Small groups share and merge ideas with the *large group.* (15 minutes)

7. **Draft Vision Narrative**

In addition to the specifics of the vision, it is important to write a narrative about what it would *look like, sound like, feel like* if the vision was being implemented in every classroom. Brainstorm ideas, at a minimum, if this piece must be delegated to the Leadership Team to finish because of time constraints.

Again, give *individuals* a chance to think. (5 minutes)

Have individuals compare and combine notes in their *small groups.* (15 minutes)

Compare and combine small group notes to *whole group.* (20 minutes)

8. **Answer Questions**

You might ask the staff to answer these questions if you have time after you finish the shared vision and school goals.

▼ What professional development is needed and when?

▼ What materials are needed to implement the vision?

▼ What other things need to be done to implement the vision?

▼ How will the implementation of the vision be supported?

▼ How can progress be measured?

ASSESSING THE IMPLEMENTATION OF THE VISION

If a vision is not monitored and measured, it is probably not being implemented. A strong vision implementation tool that reflects the specific vision of the school can be created in house. By listing the features of the vision in either a rubric structure or adding a five-point scale, you can quickly develop your own tool. Appendix B shows an example of a vision rubric.

CREATING THE SHARED VISION

Marylin Avenue Elementary School teachers and staff found that creating the shared vision was one of the most beneficial activities they completed. It was also one of the hardest. The vision helped them shift their culture, create new ways of working, and attain instructional coherence. They also found that revisiting the mission and vision, often, helped to make both truly shared.

SUMMARY

To get focused acts of improvement, schools need guiding principles to be determined, agreed upon, and committed to. These guiding principles will then lead to the development of a vision that can be truly shared and that will guide the development of action plans.

5

USING THE PROBLEM-SOLVING CYCLE TO ANALYZE CONTRIBUTING CAUSES

All staff participated in identifying contributing causes of our undesirable results. Using the Education for the Future problem-solving cycle activity helped staff engage in deep discussions and honestly think about an issue before solving it. In the past, we would identify a gap and then solve it in the same half hour. The problem-solving cycle made us think through an issue and gather data to understand it in greater depth before solving it. Staff used this activity for evaluating programs, strategies, and processes.

Marylin Avenue School

After a vision is created, and the data analyzed, staff can determine the gaps. Gaps are the difference between where the school is (data) and where it wants to be (vision).

In order to eliminate a gap, staff needs to understand the underlying reasons this gap exists. The purpose of the problem-solving cycle is to get all staff involved in thinking through a gap and understanding its origins before jumping to solutions.

The first three steps in the problem-solving cycle (Figure 5.1) are key and the focus of this activity.

PROBLEM-SOLVING CYCLE ACTIVITY

1. Establish the size of the group(s) that will be going through this activity. Small groups are beneficial in allowing everyone to participate, even if groups are working on the same problem. However, if you want whole-staff change, get the whole staff involved.

2. Start out with guidelines or ground rules of acceptable and unacceptable behavior, and how they will be monitored. Make sure it is a "safe" room for threat-free, honest, open discussion.

3. Have the group clearly identify a problem to be solved, or gap to be understood, stated in objective terms. For example, *Not all students are reading at grade level by grade three,* as opposed to, 40 percent of our students are not capable of reading by grade three. The problem should let you find the data, as opposed to presenting the data.

4. Brainstorm hunches and hypotheses about why the problem exists (takes about ten minutes). This can spell out what teachers are thinking about the problem currently.

5. Considering the problem, identify questions that need to be answered to find out more about the problem (e.g., How many students have not been reading on grade level by grade three for the past three years?)

Figure 5.1
Problem-Solving Cycle

Steps in Solving a Problem

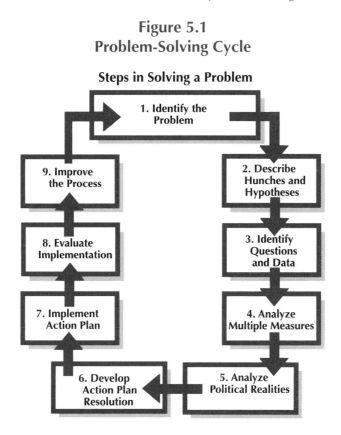

6. For each question, determine the data that need to be gathered to answer the question. This list becomes the data analysis. Eye-balling this list, one can see that for the most part, the data will fall into the four categories of demographics, student learning, perceptions, and school processes.

7. Gather and analyze the data. If you can, look at other subject areas while researching the area in question. They often require the same attention and as long as you are analyzing the data, do all subjects.

8. Continue with the problem-solving cycle through action planning and implementation.

Debriefing the Problem-Solving Cycle Activity

The Problem: First of all, the statement *Not all students are reading on grade level by grade three* is not a "problem." It is the result of our current processes. If we want different results, we must change the processes that create the results.

The Hunches: If you are not using data to solve your "problem," your staff is probably using these hunches, because this is what the staff believes is the reason the problem exists. The first few hunches in this exercise will be excuses or frustrations, like "the parents don't care" and "the kid is not trying." It is very good to get these out in the open. You ultimately will be able to collect data to determine if these hunches are fact or fiction. (Hopefully, you will be able to put the fiction to rest and concentrate on the facts.) As staff members continue to brainstorm, you start hearing things like, "but that is not the way we teach reading" and "maybe we should agree on what we are doing to teach reading" – very powerful discussions.

Staff will see quickly that the first few hunches are not the reasons for the undesirable results. By the time staff members get to 15 and 16 hunches, their thinking becomes deeply inward about what they are doing to get these results. The last four reasons are probably as close to the contributing causes as we are likely to get.

Questions and Data: When you get to the questions and data, most staffs will say, "What are the answers to those questions? We need the data before we can solve this problem . . . and we need the answers now!"

The data that the staff will be asking for are very powerful. Through this activity, they are giving permission to look at data you would have difficulty getting to in other ways, such as looking at student achievement results by classroom. While we are at it, look at math and writing to see if the reading results are related to these areas.

Very logically, staff will have covered the four circles in their questions that must be answered with data before solving the problem. In other words, the types of questions and data the staff is listing will require looking at demographics, perceptions, student learning, and school processes. We merely need to get the data to staff.

USING THE PROBLEM-SOLVING CYCLE

Marylin Avenue found that the problem-solving-cycle activity was a quick, easy, and fun way to investigate emotionally charged issues. All staff get a say in why the "problem" exists which gives them a vested interest in using the results. Marylin Avenue staff became adept in using this process and used it to evaluate programs.

SUMMARY

The problem-solving cycle is a wonderful activity for getting all staff involved in understanding more about an undesirable result before coming up with a solution that will keep getting the same results unless staff think and act differently. The problem-solving cycle gets staffs talking about their processes and practices, and ultimately leads to changing processes and practices that are not working and enhancing the ones that are working.

6

STRATEGIES TO IMPLEMENT THE VISION

We engaged in schoolwide professional learning in assessment and instructional strategies. We wanted teachers to work differently, so we had to support their continual learning of new assessment and instructional strategies.

We began using common assessments to clarify where students were at any time during the year.

We established collaborative teams, and meeting times were enforced. Teams used the time to discuss student assessment results and student work and how to change instructional strategies to get improved results. We kept these times sacred and modeled how to use the time and data effectively.

We shifted our focus from teaching to learning.

Marylin Avenue School

Marylin Avenue Elementary School staff members modeled collecting data and using the data to inform decisions when they determined what professional learning their teachers needed. They used the continuous improvement framework shown in Figure 6.1, and described below, to determine strategies needed to implement the vision.

CONTINUOUS IMPROVEMENT PLANNING

Basically, five big, but very logical, questions must be answered with data to create a plan that will make a difference for all students and all teachers, and to get student achievement increases across the board in one year. These questions are:

▼ *Where are we now?*

▼ *Where do we want to be?*

▼ *How did we get to where we are now?*

▼ *How are we going to get to where we want to be?*

▼ *How will we know if what we are doing is making a difference?*

These questions are described on the pages that follow, along with the rationale for why it is important to look at the data reflected in these questions.

WHERE ARE WE NOW?

Knowing where we are now is the part of continuous improvement planning that requires a comprehensive and honest look at all the school's data—not just student learning results. This helps staff reflect on how the school is getting its results. Four sub questions need to be answered about *Where are we now?* (Introduced in Chapters 2 and 3.)

Figure 6.1
Continuous Improvement Planning

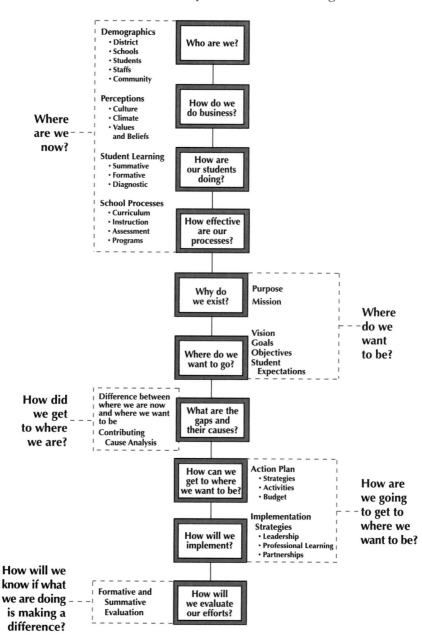

Who Are We?

Continuous school improvement planning begins by asking a question that can be answered with demographic data: *Who are we?* Specifically—

▼ *Who are the students?*

▼ *Who is the staff?*

▼ *Who is the community?*

The answers to these questions are important to the understanding of the demographic characteristics of the school, students, staff, and community in order to establish the context of the classroom, school, district, and community. It is important to understand student and community populations now because it is these two groups whose needs we must meet. It is also important to know how these populations have changed over time, as these trends indicate whom the school will be serving in the future, which, in turn, helps inform plans for the future. This information can also help teachers understand their professional learning needs.

Staff experiences, ethnicity, gender, languages spoken, certification, levels of education, longevity within the system, and plans for retirement are important data. These data can help schools place appropriate teachers with students, hire strategically and effectively, and ensure that a continuum of learning is possible. Demographic changes can also help explain student achievement results. All of these data must be considered as staff members create a continuous improvement plan.

Attendance, behavior, and program enrollment data are demographic data that provide information about our students, as well as give us insight into our leadership philosophies and how we move students within our system.

How Do We Do Business?

The question, *How do we do business?*, is answered through data gathered to assess the school's culture, climate, and organizational processes. Perceptual data, organizational processes, and values and beliefs fall into this category. Staff values and beliefs, most often assessed through questionnaires and/or determined during visioning processes, can tell a staff if team building or specific professional learning is necessary. These data can also advise us as to what is possible to implement. For example, if in a questionnaire staff members report that they believe there is no vision or that certain aspects of the vision will not improve student learning, they need to revisit the vision before they can implement anything new. If staff is not collaborating now, a plan that relies on heavy collaborative processes must first provide for the attainment of collaboration and communication skills and a clear structure to get everyone understanding expectations.

Student and parent questionnaires can add different perspectives to the information generated from staff data about how the school does business. Students can report what it takes for them to learn and how they are being taught. A school might have extensive plans to improve parent involvement without considering that parents do not feel welcome in the school. A schoolwide self-assessment can provide an overview of where the staff believes the school is on the measures that make a difference for continuous school improvement. These assessments often surprise administrators who think all staff members are thinking about school in the same way. If a school staff does not know how it really does business, it could be creating plans that might never be implemented.

How Are Our Students Doing?

The next data question, *How are our students doing?*, requires a synthesis of student learning data in all subject areas, disaggregated by all student groups. These data ensure that we are meeting the needs of all student groups and uncovering strengths and areas for improvement. In this category, teachers and other staff members must be clear as to what they want students to know and be able to do. What students know and are able to do as they begin the grade, semester, course, or unit will help teachers target their instruction. Formative assessments should be used to monitor student learning and to make sure the instructional processes are effective. These formative assessments should predict the summative measures of standards attainment.

How Effective Are Our Processes?

School processes include curriculum, instruction and assessment strategies, leadership, programs, and processes. These are the elements of our organizations over which we have almost complete control, but which we tend to measure the least. Answering this question calls for a complete accounting of all programs and processes operating throughout the learning organization, along with an assessment and evaluation of their effectiveness.

Everyone on staff must understand the intent of every program and process, and know what to do when students are not learning. Processes can be mapped with flowcharting tools, and data can be used to determine if the structures are working.

WHERE DO WE WANT TO BE?

A school defines its destination through its mission, vision, goals, and standards. These fall under the umbrella of the district's vision, goals, and standards which, in turn, are aligned with the state's vision, goals, and standards. One can determine how effectively the mission and vision are being implemented through the data gathered.

Why Do We Exist?

Why do we exist can be answered by determining the purpose of the school. The mission is the "public" version of the purpose. If staff members do not agree on one purpose, there are multiple purposes being used, resulting in a lack of continuity and instructional coherence.

Where Do We Want to Go?

The school vision spells out how the purpose and mission will be carried out. The more specific the vision, with respect to curriculum, instruction, assessment, and environment, the better the chances are that the vision will be implemented by everyone in the organization. A narrative vision, in addition to the specifics, helps staff know what the learning organization will look like, sound like, and feel like when the vision is implemented.

What Are the Gaps and Their Causes?

Gaps are the differences between *Where are we now* and *Where we want to be.* Gaps are determined by synthesizing the differences in the results the school is getting with its current processes, and the results the school wants to get for its students. It is important to dig deeply into each gap to uncover contributing causes, or the gap cannot be eliminated.

HOW DID WE GET TO WHERE WE ARE?

Gap analysis tells schools how far away they are from their visions. Contributing cause analyses, along with the data analyses, can help schools understand how they got their current results, and what it will take to eliminate the gaps. Analyzing contributing causes guides understanding of how we can get to where we want to be. The resulting strategies and actions are detailed in the action plan.

HOW ARE WE GOING TO GET TO WHERE WE WANT TO BE?

The implications of the data analysis the school vision, gap analysis, and contributing cause analysis inform the plan.

How Can We Get to Where We Want to Be?

The answer to *How can we get to where we want to be?* is key to unlocking how the vision will be implemented and how gaps will be eliminated. An action plan, consisting of strategies, activities, person(s) responsible, due dates, timelines, and required resources, needs to be developed to implement and achieve the vision and goals and to eliminate the contributing causes of the gaps.

How Will We Implement?

This question refers to the structures, such as for leadership, professional learning, and partnerships that need to be in place to ensure the implementation of the vision and the action plan. The action plan includes how the vision will be implemented, monitored, evaluated, and improved. Action plans must include how and when decisions will be made, identify professional learning required to gain new skills and knowledge, and clarify the use of partners to achieve the vision.

HOW WILL WE KNOW IF WHAT WE ARE DOING IS MAKING A DIFFERENCE?

With the comprehensive data analysis complete, most of the evaluation work has been started.

How Will We Evaluate Our Efforts?

Ongoing evaluation is required to assess the alignment of all parts of the system to the vision and the results the learning organization is getting. Evaluation needs to be designed before implementation, not only at the end, to know if what a school is doing is making a difference for students. Evaluation questions to consider are *What do we want to result from this program, process, or plan? How can we measure, and how will we know it is making the intended difference?*

IMPLEMENTING THE VISION

Marylin Avenue Elementary School used the *Continuous Improvement Planning* framework to create its action plan, and incorporated a shared decision-making structure that ensured the staff would collaborate using formative assessments and student work. Together staff members agreed to staffwide professional learning that would help them implement the vision and get instructional coherence. The plan also included a true partnership with parents and an evaluation plan that informed them about how they were doing along the way.

SUMMARY

When schools honestly answer the questions in the continuous improvement framework, the implications for the continuous improvement plan become obvious. The strategies that need to be put into place to get student achievement increases at every grade level, in every subject area, and with every student become clear to everyone.

7

CREATING A
SCHOOL PORTFOLIO

*As a part of our follow-up to the
2006 Summer Institute, we began the creation of a
School Portfolio to house our data, vision, and plan.
The School Portfolio helps us assess where we are
at any time with respect to our vision. The Portfolio
provides the focus and the sense of urgency to improve.*

Marylin Avenue School

THE SCHOOL PORTFOLIO

The School Portfolio (AKA *The Continuous Improvement Portfolio*) provides a uniquely appropriate and effective framework for describing current processes, and for planning, monitoring, and evaluating schoolwide improvement efforts. This Portfolio is a comprehensive framework for continuous improvement, a self-assessment tool, a process, and a communication product. It describes efforts to engender and maintain systemic and continuous schoolwide improvement and documents a school's vision, goals, plans, and progress. School Portfolios evolve, grow, improve, and enable schools to make better decisions. They guide the improvement of what is most important to schools and reflect the complexity of each unique school organization. The School Portfolio focuses the evaluation of schools—which are by nature complex organizations—by offering a means to monitor the parts and their interrelationships as they compose the whole. This framework is designed to work for accreditations, compliance reviews, schoolwide and program evaluations, and grant proposals. If kept up-to-date, schools will be ready for regulatory audits and can, therefore, continue their important continuous improvement work to meet the academic needs of students.

The components of the School Portfolio are:
- ▼ Information and Analysis
- ▼ Student Achievement
- ▼ Quality Planning
- ▼ Leadership
- ▼ Professional Learning
- ▼ Partnership Development
- ▼ Continuous Improvement and Evaluation

Each of these components has a continuum, as described in Chapter 3 and shown in Appendix A, that allows schools to understand where they are, as a staff, with respect to their approach, implementation and outcomes, and encourages them to set goals for improvement.

Information and Analysis is a critical element in planning for change and in supporting continuous schoolwide improvement. Schools must analyze existing data and collect additional information to understand how to meet the needs of their students, to understand the contributing causes of problems or undesirable results, to assess growth, and to predict the types of educational programs that will be needed in the future. The intent of this section is to establish systematic and rigorous reliance on data for decision making in all parts of the organization. This section answers the question, *Where are we now?*

Student Achievement describes strategies for increasing student achievement—the school's "Constancy of Purpose." The intent of this component is to support schools in moving from a fire-fighting approach to one of systemic *prevention* of student failure; to help turn teachers who provide information into facilitators who understand and can predict the impact of their actions on student achievement; and to facilitate efforts to change students from recipients of knowledge delivery to goal setting self-assessors who produce independent, quality work. This section of the School Portfolio describes *Where we want to be,* as well as what it would be like if we got there.

Quality Planning by schools must be strategic, or change efforts will not be implemented. A well-defined and well-executed schoolwide improvement effort is based on a strategic action plan that provides a logical direction for change and lays out the action to the vision. This component assists schools in developing the elements of a strategic plan, taking the mission that describes the purpose of the school; a vision that represents the long-range goals of the school; goals that promote the vision; gap and contributing cause analyses; and creating an action plan—procedural steps needed to implement the goals, including timelines, resources, and accountability; outcome measures; and a plan for continuous improvement and evaluation. The plan and the evaluation of the plan appear in this section, and answer the questions, *What are the gaps?* and *How can we get to where we want to be?*

The next three sections of the School Portfolio evolve from the plan and answer the question, *How will we implement?*

Professional Learning helps staff members, teachers, and principals change the manner in which they work—how they make decisions; gather, analyze, and utilize data; plan, teach, and monitor achievement; evaluate personnel; and assess the impact of new approaches to instruction and assessment on students. Professional learning provides individuals with opportunities to improve their personal performance on a continuous basis and to learn new skills for working with each other in reforming their culture and workplace. Procedures, plans, and calendars for the above appear in this section of a School Portfolio.

Leadership focuses on creating a learning environment that encourages everyone to contribute to making school have a cumulative, purposeful effect on all students' learning. A quality leadership infrastructure emphasizes the prevention of problems—such as student failure—as opposed to short-term solving or covering up of problems, and makes the schoolwide change effort conceivable in a school. Leadership assists schools in thinking through shared decision making and structures that will work with their specific population, climate, and vision. Leaders must understand that their job is to help everyone in the organization implement the vision. The leadership structure is the backbone of the continuous improvement process. Details, roles, and responsibilities are housed in this section of the continuous improvement portfolio.

Partnership Development with the school's community must benefit all partners. Schools know that parents, the community, and businesses are important to their vision. They also realize that parents, community members, and businesses want to contribute to schools; they just need to know how. *Partnership Development* is about starting with what schools expect students to know and be able to do, and then inviting parents, community, and businesses to plan with them for how they can all work together to that end. This section of the portfolio brings partnerships alive. This is where the partnership plan resides and partnership stories are told.

Finally, schools need to know if what they are doing is making a difference before the end of the year. This final section of the School Portfolio is about formative and summative evaluation of all aspects of the learning organization.

Continuous Improvement and Evaluation of all operations of the school is essential to schools seeking improvement in the manner in which they do business. *Continuous Improvement and Evaluation* assists schools in further understanding the interrelationships of the components of continuous improvement and in improving their processes and products on an ongoing basis. Schools committed to the School Portfolio approach and to schoolwide improvement assess their progress each year on each of the seven continuums described in Chapter 3 and shown in Appendix A and then chart the progress made in their Portfolios. This assessment process brings all the staff members together to shape and maintain their shared vision and provides motivation for the continuous improvement of all elements of the school.

With the *Continuous Improvement Continuums* as a base, the School Portfolio has all of the characteristics common to measurements used to create successful organizations as defined by Tom Peters in *Thriving on Chaos:*[1]

▼ *a simple presentation*—easy to read and understand text, graphs, and charts, available for viewing by interested parties at any time

▼ *visible measurements*—located in the portfolio, developed, or adopted by staff

▼ *everyone's involvement*—in the design and development, in activities described within, and in keeping it current

▼ *an undistorted collection of primary information*—such as longitudinal data and examples of student work

▼ *a straightforward measurement approach*—using a combination of criteria and outcomes that explicitly describe what is important and what is to be measured by school staff

▼ *an overall feel of urgency and perpetual improvement*— which results from the discrepancy between where the school is and where the school wants to be, and from a sense of accountability on the part of the staff to move the school to where it wants to be (to show academic improvement) with all children.

The intent of the work of the School Portfolio is not to have schools start over with their continuous improvement efforts. The intent is to pull together elements of work that the school has completed, and is

---

[1]Peters, Tom (1987). *Thriving on Chaos: Handbook for a Management Revolution.* New York: NY: HarperCollins.

in the process of completing, into one efficient document that lives on. We want schools to start wherever they are and with whatever they have. We also want schools to continue on their improvement journeys for a long time, measure their progress along the way, and make the progress they desire. One of the unique features of the School Portfolio is that it is a product and a process. This means that no matter where your staffs are with respect to continuous improvement, no matter what has been done, there is an entering point that will fit your situation.

CREATING AND UPDATING THE SCHOOL PORTFOLIO

Below is what Marylin Avenue Elementary put in its School Portfolio in the first year:

Information and Analysis	Data profile (Chapters 1 and 2)
Student Achievement	Vision (Chapter 4)
Quality Planning	Gap analysis, contributing cause analysis (Chapter 5) and the action plan
Professional Learning	Professional learning calendar, created from the plan and leadership structure (Chapter 6)
Leadership	Leadership structure, including when staff would collaborate (Chapter 6)
Partnership Development	What the school is doing with and for parents and community to achieve student outcomes
Continuous Improvement and Evaluation	Results of the *Continuous Improvement Continuums* (Chapter 3) and reflections of the alignment of the parts to the whole (Chapters 6 and 7)

Marylin Avenue updates its School Portfolio each year by including new data and analyses of data. This is the most exciting part for staff, as they can see changes in all four types of data, especially student achievement and climate and culture. They also revisit their vision to make sure everyone still believes in it and that the data support it. Programs have been altered and dropped because the data did not support their operations.

Marylin staff members revisit the plan to acknowledge their accomplishments and upgrade objectives and strategies. As they update their professional learning needs, leadership structure, and partnership development, they determine what would make each of these more effective.

Each year, the *Continuous Improvement Continuums* help teachers and staff reflect on their progress in each section of the School Portfolio, to acknowledge the alignment of all parts, and to determine next steps. Marylin Avenue Elementary School houses their *Continuous Improvement Continuum* reports in the *Continuous Improvement and Evaluation* section of their School Portfolio.

SUMMARY

Because school improvement is an ongoing, complex and multifaceted process, the School Portfolio is the most appropriate and authentic means to chronicle the multidimensionality of schoolwide improvement and its development over time. Schools that use a School Portfolio benefit immensely from ownership and a shared meaning of the improvement process and its results. A School Portfolio, combined with assessment criteria, allows for a deep understanding of:

▼ the elements and processes of a school

▼ what needs to be improved and why

▼ how the school plans to carry out the improvement efforts

▼ the expected outcomes of the approach to improvement

▼ the efforts to implement the plan

▼ the results of the effort

A School Portfolio provides a view of the big picture of all the elements and shows how they interrelate to make a whole. With a School Portfolio, it is easy to see what needs to be altered to keep the efforts progressing.

8
CONCLUSION

What Marylin Avenue Elementary staff members did to improve teaching and learning in one year: They—

1. *looked at all the school's data;*

2. *self-assessed on the Education for the Future Continuous Improvement Continuums that helped get all staff on the same page;*

3. *developed a vision to get all staff agreeing to one direction;*

4. *used a problem-solving cycle to understand contributing causes and to evaluate processes;*

5. *participated in schoolwide professional learning;*

6. *developed and used common formative assessments;*

7. *established and used collaborative teams to review student data and student work; and*

8. *created and used a School Portfolio to provide focus and the sense of urgency to improve.*

Education for the Future is convinced that if any school, whether elementary, middle, or secondary, does the eight things mentioned above and described in the preceding seven chapters, it will get student achievement increases at every grade level, in every subject area, and with every group of students in one year, and will be able to maintain those increases over time.

MARYLIN AVENUE ELEMENTARY SCHOOL
2007-08

In 2007-08, Marylin Avenue staff members continued to implement the strategies they began implementing in 2006-07, as described in this book. In addition, the staff mapped many school processes using flowcharting tools. All members of the staff understand what they are doing collectively to ensure that all students are proficient and what they need to do when students are not learning. In addition to mapping processes, the teachers and others on staff gather data related to the processes to make sure they are teaching what they intend to teach, and that they are getting the results they want and expect for all students. Marylin Avenue teachers know now when to adjust their processes and know the impact of those adjustments.

As this book goes to press, Marylin Avenue was receiving its 2007-08 preliminary accountability results. Happily, the school's results show that it is achieving instructional coherence and moving all students forward. The results again showed increases at every grade level, in every subject area, and with every student group. Marylin Avenue's API results for 2007-08 are 742, a 37-point increase. The school's target was 7.

As the table in Figure 8.1 shows, Marylin Avenue has come a long way in the past two years in improving student learning for all students. Besides the specific things mentioned in this

Figure 8.1
Marylin Avenue Elementary School
API Growth and Targets Met, 2002-03 to 2007-08

Year	Number Tested	Base	Target	Actual	Met Target
2002-03	276	681	6	1	No
2003-04	270	665	6	-17	No
2004-05	313	662	7	-5	No
2005-06	303	651	7	-7	No
2006-07	295	705	7	54	Yes
2007-08	286	742	7	37	Yes

book to get them started, Marfel Kusko, Leadership Team Leader, said[1] the reason Marylin Avenue continues to get student achievement increases is that they—

▼ *Shifted their culture,* through the use of data, committing to and implementing the vision, consistent leadership, professional learning that helped them get the results, and teacher collaboration with data;

▼ *Adopted common formative assessments,* which helped every teacher know what students know and do not know, and how to target her/his instruction;

▼ *Examined student data,* in particular common formative assessments, that allowed them to alter their instructional processes throughout the year to ensure all students' learning;

▼ *Collaborated* by grade level to review the formative data, with a focus on teaching to the standards;

▼ *Benefited from strong leadership* that never let go of the vision—modeling and supporting its implementation at every step along the way;

[1] *Education for the Future 2008 Summer Institute.*

Benefits of Doing the Work

Besides getting student achievement increases at every grade level, subject area, and with every student group two years in a row, Marylin Avenue staff members say additional benefits they are enjoying include:

▼ Improved public image

▼ Improved staff morale and commitment

▼ Improved student morale

▼ Interest from the central office and other schools in the district

▼ Interest from the County Office of Education and other schools outside the district

▼ Being featured in this book

Challenges and Next Steps for 2008-09

Continuing to get student achievement increases is hard work. Marylin Avenue teachers and administrators believe their biggest challenges for the 2008-09 school year include:

▼ *Staying focused* on the vision, the data, and the strategies put into place that work

▼ *Communication*—information dissemination, and coming to consensus

▼ *Making sure they are addressing the academic, social, emotional, and physical needs of all their students*

Next steps for 2008-09 include—

▼ Revisiting the shared vision

▼ Revising/updating the action plan

▼ Improving communication

▼ Continuing to map and measure school processes

▼ Deeply implementing the vision and the processes that work

Marylin Avenue Advice to Schools Wanting Student Achievement Increases

Schools wanting student achievement increases at every grade level, subject area, and with every student group should consider the following:

▼ *Gain an understanding of the continuous school improvement planning process.* Do not take short cuts. Review all your school data. Find out where your school really is with school improvement. Improve from that point, not from where you think your school is.

▼ *Get a shared vision.* Get a specific vision so everyone understands what is expected with respect to curriculum, instruction, assessment, collaboration, environment; and really share it, meaning that everyone understands the vision in the same way and is committed to implementing all aspects of it. It is necessary to continually revisit the vision. It is not a one-time deal.

▼ *Share knowledge.* As we began, and continue, on our continuous school improvement journey, we all have become readers of the research about what works in classrooms and schools. If we are not reading to learn about what works, we are just doing the same things over and over. Not everyone can read everything, so we need ways to share and to translate the learnings into our real life.

▼ *Share leadership.* Our leadership structure ensures that we are all leaders at this school, with our main job being to help each other implement the vision and gain student learning results for all students.

▼ *Share practice.* There is no benefit to keeping classroom strategies secret. We all become smarter when we share and work together.

▼ *Learn by doing.* Sometimes we just have to give new strategies our best try, share, study the implementation, adjust, try again, and share.

ADVICE TO PROFESSIONAL LEARNING COORDINATORS

Too many schools are being told they "already know what needs to improve, just focus on one thing at a time." If you want your school to get student achievement increases in every subject area, at every grade level, and with every student group, you must be looking at big picture data and vision, and truly understand what is being implemented to know what needs to change.

Please do not allow your schools to focus on just one thing they think can change—look at all the data. Schools are generating and gathering all sorts of data. Review all the data, understand the data, and look for commonalities. Look for leverage points. Listen to the students, staff, and parents.

Look beyond summative student achievement scores. Schools that look only at summative student achievement scores tend to work to fix the kids without looking to fix their own processes. The systems thinking scholars would tell us that 80% of what needs to change is us—our processes. We need to look at data along the way so we can adjust.

ADVICE TO DISTRICT ADMINISTRATORS

Allow your schools to engage in their own continuous improvement efforts if they have good structures in mind, are documenting and measuring implementation, and if they are able to show progress. Requiring individual schools to conform to a district approach is not always the right answer. Continuous improvement should be about each school's characteristics, vision, processes, and results. While we are not professing allowing "pockets of wonderfulness" to emerge, we are suggesting not holding back schools that have a plausible framework in mind, with a strong leader to implement it.

Get all your schools looking at all their data, creating a vision, using one plan that is based on what the data are saying to implement that vision, monitoring and measuring their assessment and instructional strategies, and collaborating with each other to achieve instructional coherence. A continuous improvement framework can be a tremendous help to this end.

SUMMARY

Marylin Avenue Elementary School is a typical California school with a student population that has become increasingly English language learners, qualifiers for free/reduced lunch, and decreasingly Caucasian, with a teaching faculty that is mostly Caucasian. In spite of these challenging population changes, staff was able to improve student achievement results at every grade level, in every subject area, and with every subgroup of students two years in a row. With data and process tools, staff was able to see where the school was and to use that information to get all staff on the same page to implement a vision and to engage in powerful professional learning and collaboration strategies. Marylin Avenue staff will continue to use the continuous improvement framework and monitor and measure processes to ensure that all students are learning.

The framework which this school used for continuous improvement can be used by any school or learning organization. It is the use of the entire framework that makes the difference, starting with the data.

APPENDIX A
CONTINUOUS IMPROVEMENT
CONTINUUMS FOR
SCHOOLS AND DISTRICTS

School Continuous Improvement Continuum
INFORMATION AND ANALYSIS

	One	Two	Three
Approach	Data or information about student performance and needs are not gathered in any systematic way; there is no way to determine what needs to change at the school, or classroom levels, based on data.	There is no systematic process, but some teacher and student information is collected and used to problem solve.	School collects data related to student performance (e.g., attendance, enrollment, achievement) and conducts surveys on student, teacher, and parent needs. The information is used to drive the strategic quality plan for school change.
Implementation	No information is gathered with which to make changes. Student dissatisfaction with the learning process is seen as an irritation, not a need for improvement.	Some data are tracked, such as attendance, drop-out rates, and enrollment. Only a few individuals are asked for feedback about areas of schooling.	School collects information on current and former students (e.g., demographics, student learning, and perceptions), analyzes and uses it in conjunction with future trends for planning.
Outcome	Only anecdotal and hypothetical information are available about student performance, behavior, and perceptions. Problems are solved individually with short-term results.	Little data are available. Change is limited to some areas of the school depending upon individual teachers and their efforts.	Information collected about student and parent needs, assessment, and instructional practices is shared with the school staff and used to plan for change. Information helps staff understand pressing issues, and track results for improvement.

School Continuous Improvement Continuum
INFORMATION AND ANALYSIS

Four	Five	
There is systematic and systemic reliance on data (including data for all student groups) as a basis for decision making at the classroom level as well as at the school level. Changes are based on the study of data to meet the needs of students and teachers.	Information is gathered in all areas of student interaction with the school throughout the school year. Teachers engage students in gathering information on their own performance. Accessible to all levels, data are comprehensive in scope and an accurate reflection of school quality.	**Approach**
Data, including school processes, are used to improve the effectiveness of teaching strategies on all student learning. Students' historical performances are graphed and utilized for diagnostics. Student evaluations and performances are analyzed and used by teachers in all classrooms to continually improve instruction. Contributing causes are analyzed.	Innovative teaching processes that meet the needs of students are implemented to the delight of teachers, parents, and students. Information is analyzed and used to prevent student failure, and to evaluate all processes and programs. Contributing causes are known through analyses. Problems are prevented through the use of data.	**Implementation**
A data system is in place. Positive trends begin to appear in most classrooms and schoolwide. There is evidence that these results are caused by understanding and effectively using data, including analyzing for contributing causes.	Students are delighted with the school's instructional processes and proud of their own capabilities to learn and assess their own growth. Good to excellent achievement is the result for all students. No student falls through the cracks. Teachers use data to predict and prevent potential problems. Schoolwide, only "effective" processes and programs are used.	**Outcome**

School Continuous Improvement Continuum
STUDENT ACHIEVEMENT

	One	Two	Three
Approach	Instructional and organizational processes critical to student success are not identified. Little distinction of student learning differences is made. Some teachers believe that not all students can achieve.	Some data are collected on student background and performance trends. Learning gaps are noted to direct improvement of instruction. It is known that student learning standards must be used.	Student learning standards are identified, and a continuum of learning is created throughout the school. Student performance data are collected and compared to the standards in order to analyze how to improve learning for all students.
Implementation	All students are taught the same way. There is no communication with students about their academic needs or learning styles. There are no analyses of how to improve instruction.	Some effort is made to track and analyze student achievement trends on a school-wide basis. Teachers begin to understand the needs and learning gaps of students.	Teachers study effective instruction and assessment strategies to implement standards and to increase their students' learning. Student feedback and analysis of achievement data are used in conjunction with implementation support strategies.
Outcome	There is wide variation in student attitudes and achievement with undesirable results. There is high dissatisfaction among students with learning. Student background is used as an excuse for low student achievement.	There is some evidence that student achievement trends are available to teachers and are being used. There is much effort, but minimal observable results, in improving student achievement.	There is an increase in communication between students and teachers regarding student learning. Teachers learn about effective instructional strategies that will implement the shared vision, including student learning standards, and meet the needs of their students. They make some gains.

School Continuous Improvement Continuum
STUDENT ACHIEVEMENT

Four	Five	
Formative and summative data on student achievement are used throughout the school to pursue the improvement of student learning. Teachers collaborate to implement appropriate instruction and assessment strategies for meeting student learning standards articulated across grade levels. All teachers believe that all students can learn.	School makes an effort to exceed student achievement expectations. Innovative instructional changes are made to anticipate learning needs and improve student achievement. Teachers are able to predict characteristics impacting student achievement and to know how to perform from a small set of internal quality measures to ensure success.	**Approach**
There is a systematic focus on implementing student learning standards and on the improvement of student learning schoolwide. Effective instruction and assessment strategies are implemented in each classroom. Teachers collaborate and support one another with peer coaching and/or action research focused on implementing instructional strategies that lead to increased achievement and the attainment of the shared vision.	All teachers correlate critical instructional and assessment strategies with objective indicators of quality student achievement. A comparative analysis of actual individual student performance to student learning standards is utilized to adjust teaching strategies to ensure a progression of learning for all students.	**Implementation**
Increased student achievement is evident schoolwide. Student morale, attendance, and behavior are good. Teacher morale and attendance are good. Teachers converse often with each other about preventing student failure. Areas for further attention are clear.	Students and teachers conduct self-assessments to continuously improve performance. Improvements in student achievement are evident and clearly caused by teachers' and students' understandings of individual student learning standards, linked to appropriate and effective instructional and assessment strategies. A continuum of learning results. No student falls through the cracks.	**Outcome**

School Continuous Improvement Continuum
QUALITY PLANNING

	One	Two	Three
Approach	No quality plan or process exists. Data are neither used nor considered important in planning.	Staff realize the importance of reviewing data, a mission, vision, and one comprehensive action plan. Staff develop goals and timelines, and resources are allocated to begin the process of strategic planning.	A comprehensive school plan to achieve the vision is developed. Plan includes evaluation and continuous improvement.
Implementation	There is no knowledge of or direction for quality planning. Budget is allocated on an as-needed basis. Many plans exist.	School staff begins continuous improvement planning efforts by reviewing all data, laying out major steps to a shared vision, by identifying values and beliefs, the purpose of the school, a mission, vision, and student learning expectations.	Implementation goals, responsibilities, due dates, and timelines are spelled out. Support structures for implementing the plan are set in place.
Outcome	There is no evidence of comprehensive planning. Staff work is carried out in isolation. A continuum of learning for students is absent.	The school staff understands the benefits of working together to implement a comprehensive continuous improvement plan.	There is evidence that the school plan is being implemented in some areas of the school. Improvements are neither systematic nor integrated schoolwide.

School Continuous Improvement Continuum
QUALITY PLANNING

Four	Five	
One focused and integrated schoolwide plan for implementing a continuous improvement process is put into action. All school efforts are focused on the implementation of this plan that represents the achievement of the school vision.	A plan for the continuous improvement of the school, with a focus on students, is put into place. There is excellent articulation and integration of all elements in the school due to quality planning. Leadership team ensures all elements are implemented by all appropriate parties.	Approach
The quality plan is implemented through effective procedures in all areas of the school. Everyone commits to implementing the plan aligned to the vision, mission, and values and beliefs. All share responsibility for accomplishing school goals.	Schoolwide goals, mission, vision, and student learning standards are shared and articulated throughout the school and with feeder schools. The attainment of identified student learning standards is linked to planning and implementation of effective instruction that meets students' needs. Leaders at all levels are developing expertise because quality planning is the norm.	Implementation
A schoolwide plan is known to all. Results from working toward the quality improvement goals are evident throughout the school. Planning is ongoing and inclusive of all stakeholders.	Evidence of effective teaching and learning results in significant improvement of student achievement attributed to quality planning at all levels of the school organization. Teachers and administrators understand and share the school mission and vision. Quality planning is seamless and all demonstrate evidence of accountability.	Outcome

School Continuous Improvement Continuum
PROFESSIONAL LEARNING

	One	Two	Three
Approach	There is no professional learning. Teachers, principals, and staff are seen as interchangeable parts that can be replaced. Professional learning is external and usually equated to attending a conference alone. Hierarchy determines "haves" and "have-nots."	The "cafeteria" approach to professional learning is used, whereby individual teachers choose what they want to take, without regard to an overall school plan.	The shared vision, school plan, and student needs are used to target focused professional learning for all employees. Staff is inserviced on relevant instructional and leadership strategies.
Implementation	Teacher, principal, and staff performance is controlled and inspected. Performance evaluations are used to detect mistakes.	Teacher professional learning is sporadic and unfocused, lacking an approach for implementing new procedures and processes. Some leadership training begins to take place.	Teachers are involved in year-round quality professional learning. The school staff is trained in shared decision making, team-building concepts, effective communication and collaboration strategies, and data analysis at the classroom level.
Outcome	There is no professional growth and no staff or student performance improvement. There exists a high turnover rate of employees, especially administrators. Attitudes and approaches filter down to students.	The effectiveness of professional learning is not known or analyzed. Teachers feel helpless about making schoolwide changes.	Teachers, working in teams, feel supported and begin to feel they can make changes. Evidence shows that shared decision making works.

School Continuous Improvement Continuum
PROFESSIONAL LEARNING

Four	Five	
Professional learning, data-gathering methods and collaboration are used by all teachers and are directed toward the goals of the shared vision and the continuous improvement of the school. Teachers have ongoing conversations about student achievement data. All staff members receive training in their content areas. Systems thinking is considered in all decisions.	Leadership and staff continuously improve all aspects of the learning organization through an innovative, data-driven, and comprehensive continuous improvement process that prevents student failures. Effective job-embedded professional learning is ongoing for implementing the vision for student success. Traditional teacher evaluations are replaced by collegial coaching and action research focused on student learning standards. Policies set professional learning as a priority budget line-item. Professional learning is planned, aligned, and lead to the achievement of student learning standards.	Approach
Teachers, in teams, continuously set and implement student achievement goals. Leadership considers these goals and provides necessary support structures for collaboration. Teachers utilize effective support approaches as they implement new instruction and assessment strategies. Coaching and feedback structures are in place. Use of new knowledge and skills is evident.	Teams passionately support each other in the pursuit of quality improvement at all levels. Teachers make bold changes in instruction and assessment strategies focused on student learning standards and student learning styles. A teacher as action researcher model is implemented. Staffwide conversations focus on systemic reflection and improvement. Teachers are strong leaders.	Implementation
A collegial school is evident. Effective classroom strategies are practiced, articulated schoolwide, are reflective of professional learning aimed at ensuring student achievement, and the implementation of the shared vision, that includes student learning standards.	True systemic change and improved student achievement result because teachers are knowledgeable of and implement effective, differentiated teaching strategies and formative assessments for individual student learning gains. Teachers' repertoire of skills are enhanced, and students are achieving. Professional learning is driving learning at all levels. A continuum of learning exists.	Outcome

School Continuous Improvement Continuum
LEADERSHIP

	One	Two	Three
Approach	Principal as decision maker. Decisions are reactive to state, district, and federal mandates. There is no knowledge of continuous improvement.	A shared decision-making structure is put into place and discussions begin on how to achieve a school vision. Most decisions are focused on solving problems and are reactive.	Leadership team is committed to continuous improvement. Leadership seeks inclusion of all school sectors and supports collaborative teams by making time provisions for their work.
Implementation	Principal makes all decisions, with little or no input from teachers, the community, or students. Leadership inspects for mistakes.	School values and beliefs are identified; the purpose of school is defined; a school mission and student learning standards are developed with representative input. A structure for studying approaches to achieving student learning standards is established.	Leadership team is active on collaborative teams and integrates recommendations from the teams' research and analyses to form a comprehensive plan for continuous improvement within the context of the school mission. Everyone is kept informed.
Outcome	Decisions lack focus and consistency. There is no evidence of staff commitment to a shared vision. Students and parents do not feel they are being heard. Decision-making process is clear and known.	The mission provides a focus for all school improvement and guides the action to the vision. The school community is committed to continuous improvement. Quality leadership techniques are used sporadically.	Leadership team is seen as committed to planning and quality improvement. Critical areas for improvement are identified. Faculty feel included in shared decision making.

School Continuous Improvement Continuum
LEADERSHIP

Four	Five	
Leadership team represents a true shared decision-making structure. Collaborative teams are reconstructed to ensure the implementation of a comprehensive continuous improvement plan.	A strong continuous improvement structure is set into place that allows for input from all sectors of the school, district, and community, ensuring strong communication, flexibility, and refinement of approach and beliefs. The school vision is student focused, based on data, and appropriate for school/community values, and meeting student needs.	**Approach**
Decisions about budget and implementation of the vision are made within teams, by the principal, by the leadership team, and by the full staff as appropriate. All decisions are communicated to the leadership team and to the full staff.	The vision is implemented and articulated across all grade levels and into feeder schools. Quality standards are reinforced throughout the school. All members of the school community understand and apply the quality standards. The leadership team has systematic interactions and involvement with district administrators, teachers, parents, community, and students about the school's direction. Necessary resources are available to implement and measure staff learning related to student learning standards.	**Implementation**
There is evidence that the leadership team listens to all levels of the organization. Implementation of the continuous improvement plan is linked to student learning standards and the guiding principles of the school. Leadership capacities for implementing the vision among teachers are evident.	Site-based management and shared decision making truly exists. Teachers understand and display an intimate knowledge of how the school operates. Teachers support and communicate with each other in the implementation of quality strategies. Teachers implement the vision in their classrooms and can determine how their new approach meets student needs and leads to the attainment of student learning standards. Leaders are standards-driven at all levels.	**Outcome**

School Continuous Improvement Continuum
PARTNERSHIP DEVELOPMENT

	One	Two	Three
Approach	There is no system for input from parents, business, or community. Status quo is desired for managing the school.	Partnerships are sought, but mostly for money and things.	School has knowledge of why partnerships are important and seeks to include businesses and parents in a strategic fashion related to student learning standards for increased student achievement.
Implementation	Barriers are erected to close out involvement of outsiders. Outsiders are managed for least impact on status quo.	A team is assigned to get partners and to receive input from parents, the community, and business in the school.	Involvement of business, community, and parents begins to take place in some classrooms and after school hours related to the vision. Partners begin to realize how they can support each other in achieving school goals. School staff understand what partners need from the partnership.
Outcome	There is little or no involvement of parents, business, or community at-large. School is a closed, isolated system.	Much effort is given to establishing partnerships. Some spotty trends emerge, such as receiving donated equipment.	Some substantial gains are achieved in implementing partnerships. Some student achievement increases can be attributed to this involvement.

School Continuous Improvement Continuum
PARTNERSHIP DEVELOPMENT

Four	Five	
School seeks effective win-win business and community partnerships and parent involvement to implement the vision. Desired outcomes are clearly identified. A solid plan for partnership development exists.	Community, parent, and business partnerships become integrated across all student groupings. The benefits of outside involvement are known by all. Parent and business involvement in student learning is refined. Student learning *regularly* takes place beyond the school walls.	Approach
There is a systematic utilization of parents, community, and businesses schoolwide. Areas in which the active use of these partnerships benefit student learning are clear.	Partnership development is articulated across all student groupings. Parents, community, business, and educators work together in an innovative fashion to increase student learning and to prepare students for the 21st Century. Partnerships are evaluated for continuous improvement.	Implementation
Gains in student satisfaction with learning and school are clearly related to partnerships. All partners benefit.	Previously non-achieving students enjoy learning with excellent achievement. Community, business, and home become common places for student learning, while school becomes a place where parents come for further education. Partnerships enhance what the school does for students.	Outcome

School Continuous Improvement Continuum
CONTINUOUS IMPROVEMENT AND EVALUATION

	One	Two	Three
Approach	Neither goals nor strategies exist for the evaluation and continuous improvement of the school organization or for elements of the school organization.	The approach to continuous improvement and evaluation is problem solving. If there are no problems, or if solutions can be made quickly, there is no need for improvement or analyses. Changes in parts of the system are not coordinated with all other parts.	Some elements of the school organization are evaluated for effectiveness. Some elements are improved on the basis of the evaluation findings.
Implementation	With no overall plan for evaluation and continuous improvement, strategies are changed by individual teachers and administrators only when something sparks the need to improve. Reactive decisions and activities are a daily mode of operation.	Isolated changes are made in some areas of the school organization in response to problem incidents. Changes are not preceded by comprehensive analyses, such as an understanding of the contributing causes of undesirable results. The effectiveness of the elements of the school organization, or changes made to the elements, is not known.	Elements of the school organization are improved on the basis of comprehensive data analyses, analysis of contributing causes of undesirable results, and the analysis of process effectiveness.
Outcome	Individuals struggle with system failure. Finger pointing and blaming others for failure occurs. The effectiveness of strategies is not known. Mistakes are repeated.	Problems are solved only temporarily and few positive changes result. Additionally, unintended and undesirable consequences often appear in other parts of the system. Many aspects of the school are incongruent, keeping the school from reaching its vision.	Evidence of effective improvement strategies is observable. Positive changes are made and maintained due to comprehensive analyses and evaluation.

Copyright © 1991–2009 Education for the Future Initiative, Chico, CA.

School Continuous Improvement Continuum
CONTINUOUS IMPROVEMENT AND EVALUATION

Four	Five	
All elements of the school's operations are evaluated for improvement and to ensure congruence of the elements with respect to the continuum of learning students experience.	All aspects of the school organization are rigorously evaluated and improved on a continuous basis. Students, and the maintenance of a continuum of learning for students, become the focus of all aspects of the school improvement process.	Approach
Continuous improvement analyses of student achievement and instructional strategies are rigorously reinforced within each classroom and across learning levels to develop a continuum of learning for students and to prevent student failure.	Comprehensive continuous improvement becomes the way of doing business at the school. Teachers continuously improve the appropriateness and effectiveness of instructional strategies based on student feedback and performance. All aspects of the school organization are improved to support teachers' efforts.	Implementation
Teachers become astute at assessing and in predicting the impact of their instructional strategies on individual student achievement. Sustainable improvements in student achievement are evident at all grade levels, due to continuous improvement.	The school becomes a congruent and effective learning organization. Only instruction and assessment strategies that produce quality student achievement are used. A true continuum of learning is in place for all students and staff. The impact of improvement is measured.	Outcome

Copyright © 1991–2009 Education for the Future Initiative, Chico, CA.

District Continuous Improvement Continuum
INFORMATION AND ANALYSIS

	One	Two	Three
Approach	Data or information about school and student performance and needs are not gathered in any systematic way. The district does not provide assistance in helping schools understand what needs to change at the school and classroom levels, based on data.	There is no systematic process for data analysis across the district. Some school, teacher, and student information are collected and used to problem solve and establish student-learning standards across the district.	School district collects data related to school and student performance (e.g., attendance, enrollment, achievement), and surveys students, staff, and parents. The information is used to drive the strategic quality plan for district and school improvement.
Implementation	No information is gathered with which to make district or school changes. Student dissatisfaction with the learning process is seen as an irritation, not a need for improvement.	Some data are tracked, such as attendance, enrollment, and drop-out rates. Only a few individuals are asked for feedback about areas of schooling and district operations.	The district collects information on current and former students (e.g., demographics, student learning, and perceptions), analyzes and uses it in conjunction with future trends for planning.
Outcome	Only anecdotal and hypothetical information are available about student performance, behavior, and perceptions. Problems are solved individually with short-term results.	Little data are available. Change is limited to some areas of the district depending upon individual administrators and their efforts.	Information collected about school needs, effective assessment, and instructional practices are shared with all school and district staff and used to plan for school and district improvement. Information helps staff understand pressing issues, and track results for improvement.operation.

District Continuous Improvement Continuum
INFORMATION AND ANALYSIS

Four	Five	
There is systematic and systemic reliance on data (including data for all student groups) as a basis for decision making at the district, school, and classroom levels. Changes are based on the study of data to meet the educational needs of students and teachers.	Information is gathered in all areas of student interaction with the school throughout the school year. The district engages administrators, teachers, and students in gathering information on their own performance. Accessible to all schools, data are comprehensive in scope and an accurate reflection of school and district quality.	Approach
Data, including school processes, are used to provide feedback to improve the effectiveness of teaching strategies on all student learning. Schools' historical data are graphed and utilized for diagnosis and leadership purposes by the district. Contributing causes are analyzed.	Innovative teaching processes that meet the needs of students are implemented across the district. Information is analyzed and used to prevent student failure and to evaluate all processes and programs. Contributing causes are known through analyses. Problems are prevented through the use of data.	Implementation
A data system is in place. Positive trends begin to appear in most schools and districtwide. There is evidence that these results are caused by understanding and effectively using the data, including the analysis of contributing causes.	Schools are delighted with their instructional processes and proud of their own capabilities to learn and assess their own growth. Good to excellent achievement is the result for all schools. Schools use data to predict and prevent potential problems. No student falls through the cracks. Districtwide, only "effective" programs are in operation.	Outcome

District Continuous Improvement Continuum
STUDENT ACHIEVEMENT

	One	Two	Three
Approach	Instructional and organizational processes critical to student success are not identified. Little distinction of student learning differences is made. Some schools believe that not all students can achieve.	Some data are collected on student background and performance trends. Learning gaps are noted to direct improvement of instruction. It is known that student learning standards must be used.	Student learning standards are identified, and a continuum of learning is created across the district. Student performance data are collected and compared to the standards in order to analyze how to improve learning for all students.
Implementation	All students are taught the same way. There is no communication between the district and schools about students' academic needs or learning styles. There are no analyses of how to improve instruction.	Some effort is made to track and analyze student achievement trends on a districtwide basis. District begins to understand the needs and learning gaps within the schools.	Teachers across the district study effective instruction and assessment strategies to implement standards and to increase students' learning. Student feedback and analysis of achievement data are used in conjunction with implementation support strategies.
Outcome	There is wide variation in student attitudes and achievement with undesirable results. There is high dissatisfaction among students with learning. Student background is used as an excuse for low student achievement.	There is some evidence that student achievement trends are available to schools and are being used. There is much effort, but minimal observable results in improving student achievement.	There is an increase in communication among district and schools, students, and teachers regarding student learning. Teachers learn about effective instructional strategies that will implement the shared vision, student learning standards, and how to meet the needs of students. The schools make some gains.

District Continuous Improvement Continuum
STUDENT ACHIEVEMENT

Four	Five	
Formative and summative data on student achievement are used throughout the district to pursue the improvement of student learning. The district ensures that teachers collaborate to implement appropriate instruction and assessment strategies for meeting student learning standards articulated across grade levels. All teachers believe that all students can learn.	The district makes an effort to exceed student achievement expectations. Innovative instructional changes are made to anticipate learning needs and improve student achievement. District makes sure that teachers are able to predict characteristics impacting student achievement and to know how to perform from a small set of internal quality measures to ensure success.	Approach
There is a systematic focus on implementing student learning standards and on the improvement of student learning districtwide. Effective instruction and assessment strategies are implemented in each school. District supports teachers supporting one another with approaches such as peer coaching and/or action research focused on implementing instruction that lead to increased achievement.	All teachers correlate critical instructional and assessment strategies with objective indicators of quality student achievement. A comparative analysis of actual individual student performance to student learning standards is utilized to adjust teaching strategies to ensure a progression of learning for all students.	Implementation
Increased student achievement is evident districtwide. The district leadership knows what it takes to support schools in improving student achievement. Student morale, attendance, and behavior are good. Teacher morale and attendance are good. Teachers converse often with each other about preventing student failure. Areas for further attention are clear.	The district, schools, and teachers conduct self-assessments to continuously improve performance. Improvements in student achievement are evident and clearly caused by teachers' and students' understandings of individual student learning standards, linked to appropriate and effective instructional and assessment strategies. A continuum of learning results. No student falls through the cracks	Outcome

District Continuous Improvement Continuum
QUALITY PLANNING

	One	Two	Three
Approach	No quality plan or process exists. Data are neither used nor considered important in planning.	The district realizes the importance of reviewing data, and having a mission, vision, and one comprehensive action plan. Staff develop goals and timelines, and resources are allocated to begin the process of strategic planning.	A comprehensive plan to achieve the district vision is developed. Plan includes evaluation and continuous improvement.
Implementation	There is no knowledge of or direction for quality planning. Budget is allocated on an as-needed basis. Many plans exist.	School district staff begins continuous improvement planning efforts by reviewing all data, laying out major steps to a shared vision, by identifying values and beliefs, the purpose of the district, a mission, vision, and student learning expectations.	Implementation goals, strategies, actions, responsibilities, due dates, and timelines are spelled out. Support structures for implementing the plan are set in place.
Outcome	There is no evidence of comprehensive planning. Staff work is carried out in isolation. A continuum of learning for students is absent.	The school district staff understands the benefits of working together to implement a comprehensive continuous improvement plan.	There is evidence that the district plan is being implemented in some areas of the district. Improvements are neither systematic nor integrated districtwide.

District Continuous Improvement Continuum
QUALITY PLANNING

Four	Five	
One focused and integrated districtwide plan for implementing a continuous improvement process is put into action. All district efforts are focused on the implementation of this plan that represents the achievement of the district vision.	A plan for the continuous improvement of the district, with a focus on students, is put into place. There is excellent articulation and integration of all elements in the district due to quality planning. Leadership team ensures all elements are implemented by all appropriate parties.	Approach
The quality management plan is implemented through effective procedures in all areas of the district. Everyone commits to implementing the plan aligned to the vision, mission, and values and beliefs. All share responsibility for accomplishing district goals.	Districtwide goals, mission, vision, and student learning standards are shared and articulated throughout the district and with feeder schools. The attainment of identified student learning standards is linked to planning and implementation of effective instruction that meets students' needs. Leaders at all levels are developing expertise because quality planning is the norm.	Implementation
A districtwide plan is known to all. Results from working toward the quality improvement goals are evident throughout the district. Planning is ongoing and inclusive of all stakeholders.	Evidence of effective teaching and learning results in significant improvement of student achievement attributed to quality planning at all levels of the district organization. Teachers and administrators understand and share the district mission and vision. Quality planning is seamless and all demonstrate evidence of accountability.	Outcome

District Continuous Improvement Continuum
PROFESSIONAL LEARNING

	One	Two	Three
Approach	There is no professional learning. Teachers, principals, and district and school staff are seen as interchangeable parts that can be replaced. Professional learning is external and usually equated to attending a conference alone. Hierarchy determines "haves" and "have-nots."	The "cafeteria" approach to professional learning is used, whereby individual teachers and administrators choose what they want to take, without regard to an overall district plan.	The shared vision, district plan and student needs are used to target focused professional learning for all employees. Staff is inserviced on relevant instructional and leadership strategies.
Implementation	District staff, principals, teachers, and school staff performance is controlled and inspected. Performance evaluations are used to detect mistakes.	Teacher professional learning is sporadic and unfocused, lacking an approach for implementing new procedures and processes. Some leadership training begins to take place.	The district ensures that teachers are involved in year-round quality professional learning. The school and district staff are trained in shared decision making, team building concepts, effective communication and collaboration strategies, and data analysis.
Outcome	There is no professional growth and no staff or student performance improvement. There exists a high turnover rate of employees, especially administrators. Attitudes and approaches filter down to teachers and students.	The effectiveness of professional learning is not known or analyzed. Teachers feel helpless and unsupported in making schoolwide changes.	Teachers, working in teams, feel supported by the district and begin to feel they can make changes. Evidence shows that shared decision making works.

District Continuous Improvement Continuum
PROFESSIONAL LEARNING

Four	Five	
Professional learning, data-gathering methods and collaboration are used by all teachers and administrators, and are directed toward the goals of the shared vision and the continuous improvement of the district and schools. Teachers have ongoing conversations about student achievement data. All staff members receive training in their content areas. Systems thinking is considered in all decisions.	Leadership and staff continuously improve all aspects of the learning organization through an innovative, data-driven, and comprehensive continuous improvement process that prevents student failures. Effective job-embedded professional learning is ongoing for implementing the vision for student success. Traditional teacher evaluations are replaced by collegial coaching and action research focused on student learning standards. Policies set professional learning as a priority budget line-item. Professional learning is planned, aligned, and leads to the achievement of student learning standards.	Approach
Teachers, in teams, continuously set and implement student achievement goals. Leadership considers these goals and provides necessary support structures for collaboration. Teachers utilize effective support approaches as they implement new instruction and assessment strategies. Coaching and feedback structures are in place. Use of new knowledge and skills is evident.	Teams passionately support each other in the pursuit of quality improvement at all levels. Teachers make bold changes in instruction and assessment strategies focused on student learning standards and student learning styles. A teacher as action researcher model is implemented. Staffwide conversations focus on systemic reflection and improvement. Administrators and teachers are strong leaders.	Implementation
A collegial school district is evident. Effective classroom strategies are practiced and articulated schoolwide. These strategies, focused on student learning standards, are reflective of professional learning aimed at ensuring student learning and the implementation of the shared vision.	True systemic change and improved student achievement result because teachers are knowledgeable of and implement effective, differentiated teaching strategies and formative assessments for individual student learning gains. Teachers' repertoire of skills is enhanced and students are achieving. Professional learning is driving learning at all levels. A continuum of learning exists in each school.	Outcome

District Continuous Improvement Continuum
LEADERSHIP

	One	Two	Three
Approach	The School Board is decision maker. Decisions are reactive to state, district, and federal mandates. There is no knowledge of continuous improvement.	A shared decision-making structure is put into place and discussions begin on how to achieve a district vision. Most decisions are focused on solving problems and are reactive.	District leadership team is committed to continuous improvement. Leadership seeks inclusion of all school sectors and supports collaborative teams by making time provisions for their work.
Implementation	The School Board makes all decisions, with little or no input from administrators, teachers, the community, or students. Leadership inspects for mistakes.	District values and beliefs are identified; the purpose of district is defined; a district mission and student learning standards are developed with representative input. A structure for studying approaches to achieving student learning standards is established.	The district leadership team is active on collaborative teams and integrates recommendations from he teams' research and analyses to form a comprehensive plan for continuous improvement within the context of the district mission. Everyone is kept informed.
Outcome	Although the decision-making process is clearly known, decisions are reactive and lack focus and consistency. There is no evidence of staff commitment to a shared vision. Students and parents do not feel they are being heard.	The mission provides a focus for all district and school improvement and guides the action to the vision. The school district community is committed to continuous improvement. Quality leadership techniques are used sporadically.	The district leadership team is seen as committed to planning and quality improvement. Critical areas for improvement are identified. District administration and school staffs feel included in shared decision making.

District Continuous Improvement Continuum
LEADERSHIP

Four	Five	
District leadership team represents a true shared decision-making structure. Collaborative teams are reconstructed for the implementation of a comprehensive continuous improvement plan.	A strong continuous improvement structure is set into place that allows for input from all sectors of the district, school, and community, ensuring strong communication, flexibility, and refinement of approach and beliefs. The district vision is student focused, based on data and appropriate for district/school/community values, and meeting student needs.	Approach
Decisions about budget and implementation of the vision are made within teams, by the school board, by the leadership team, by the individual schools, and by the full staff, as appropriate. All decisions are communicated to the leadership team and to the full staff.	The vision is implemented and articulated across all grade levels and into feeder schools. Quality standards are reinforced throughout the district. All members of the district community understand and apply the quality standards. The leadership team has systematic interactions and involvement with district administrators, teachers, parents, community, and students about the district's direction. Necessary resources are available to implement and measure staff learning related to student learning standards.	Implementation
There is evidence that the district leadership team listens to all levels of the organization. Implementation of the continuous improvement plan is linked to student learning standards and the guiding principles of the school. Leadership capacity for implementing the vision throughout the district is evident.	Site-based management and shared decision making truly exists. Teachers understand and display an intimate knowledge of how the school and district operate. Schools support and communicate with each other in the implementation of quality strategies. Teachers implement the vision in their classrooms and can determine how their new approaches meet student needs and lead to the attainment of student learning standards. Leaders are standards-driven at all levels.	Outcome

District Continuous Improvement Continuum
PARTNERSHIP DEVELOPMENT

	One	Two	Three
Approach	There is no system for input from parents, business, or community. Status quo is desired for managing the school district.	Partnerships are sought, but mostly for money and things.	School district has knowledge of why partnerships are important and seeks to include businesses and parents in a strategic fashion related to student learning standards for increased student achievement.
Implementation	Barriers are erected to close out involvement of outsiders. Outsiders are managed for least impact on status quo.	A team is assigned to get partners and to receive input from parents, the community, and business in the school district. Involvement	of business, community, and parents begins to take place in some schools and after school hours related to the vision. Partners begin to realize how they can support each other in achieving district goals. District staff understand what partners need from the partnership.
Outcome	There is little or no involvement of parents, business, or community at-large. The district is a closed, isolated system.	Much effort is given to establishing partnerships. Some spotty trends emerge, such as receiving donated equipment.	Some substantial gains are achieved in implementing partnerships. Some student achievement increases can be attributed to this involvement.

District Continuous Improvement Continuum
PARTNERSHIP DEVELOPMENT

Four	Five	
School district seeks effective win-win business and community partnerships and parent involvement to implement the vision. Desired outcomes are clearly identified. A solid plan for partnership development exists.	Community, parent, and business partnerships become integrated across all student groupings. The benefits of outside involvement are known by all. Parent and business involvement in student learning is refined. Student learning regularly takes place beyond the school and district walls.	Approach
There is systematic utilization of parents, community, and businesses districtwide. Areas in which the active use of these partnerships benefit student learning are clear.	Partnership development is articulated across all district groupings. Parents, community, business, and educators work together in an innovative fashion to increase student learning and to prepare students for the Twenty-first Century. Partnerships are evaluated for continuous improvement.	Implementation
Gains in student satisfaction with learning and school are clearly related to partnerships. All partners benefit. Previously non-achieving	students enjoy learning with excellent achievement. Community, business, and home become common places for student learning, while school becomes a place where parents come for further education. Partnerships enhance what the school district does for students.	Outcome

District Continuous Improvement Continuum
CONTINUOUS IMPROVEMENT AND EVALUATION

	One	Two	Three
Approach	Neither goals nor strategies exist for the evaluation and continuous improvement of the district organization or for elements of the organization.	The approach to continuous improvement and evaluation is problem-solving. If there are no problems, or if solutions can be made quickly, there is no need for improvement or analyses. Changes in parts of the system are not coordinated with all other parts.	Some elements of the district organization are evaluated for effectiveness. Some elements are improved on the basis of the evaluation findings.
Implementation	With no overall plan for evaluation and continuous improvement, strategies are changed by individual schools, teachers, and/or administrators only when something sparks the need to improve. Reactive decisions and activities are a daily mode of operation.	Isolated changes are made in some areas of the district organization in response to problem incidents. Changes are not preceded by comprehensive analyses, such as an understanding of the contributing causes of undesirable results. The effectiveness of the elements of the district organization is not known.	Elements of the district organization are improved on the basis of comprehensive data analyses, analyses of contributing causes of undesirable results, and the analysis of process effectiveness.
Outcome	Individuals struggle with system failure. Finger pointing and blaming others for failure occur. The effectiveness of strategies is not known. Mistakes are repeated.	Problems are solved only temporarily and few positive changes result. Additionally, unintended and undesirable consequences often appear in other parts of the system. Many aspects of the school district are incongruent, keeping the district from reaching its vision.	Evidence of effective improvement strategies is observable. Positive changes are made and maintained due to comprehensive analyses and evaluation.

District Continuous Improvement Continuum
CONTINUOUS IMPROVEMENT AND EVALUATION

Four	Five	
All elements of the district's operations are evaluated for improvement. Efforts are consistently made to ensure congruence of the elements with respect to the continuum of learning across schools.	All aspects of the district organization are rigorously evaluated and improved on a continuous basis. Students, and the maintenance of a continuum of learning for students, become the focus of all aspects of the school district improvement process.	Approach
Continuous improvement analyses of student achievement and instructional strategies are rigorously reinforced within each classroom and across learning levels to develop a continuum of learning for students and to prevent student failure.	Comprehensive continuous improvement becomes the way of doing business throughout the district. Teachers continuously improve the appropriateness and effectiveness of instructional strategies based on student feedback and performance. All aspects of the district organization are improved to support teachers' efforts.	Implementation
Teachers become astute at assessing and in predicting the impact of their instructional strategies on individual student achievement. Sustainable improvements in student achievement are evident at all grade levels due to continuous improvement supported by the district.	The district becomes a congruent and effective learning organization. Only instruction and assessment strategies that produce quality student achievement are used. A true continuum of learning is in place for all students and staff. The impact of improvements	Outcome

APPENDIX B

VISION RUBRIC EXAMPLE

BRAIN COMPATIBLE EDUCATION RUBRIC

LEVEL ONE
Physical & Social Values of Environment
• Responsibility to authority is the most important value. • Social development and interaction is based on external rewards and consequences. • The environment is agitated. • Teacher uses loud colors to display items on the bulletin board. • Students sit in rows.
Curriculum
• Subject areas and specific skills are taught in isolation. • Curriculum is textbook driven and teacher centered.
Instructional Strategies
• Textbook and lecture driven. • Students working in isolation.
Assessment
• Publishers' tests are used.
Outcomes
• Students do not see connections between school and real life and do not understand the interrelationships among concepts common to various subject areas. • Students are teacher-dependent, passive, authority complacent. • Students tend not to self-initiate.

Note: Frank Paul School Brain Compatible Education Rubrics, written by: Vickie Hagan, ITI Coach, Frank Paul School; Jackie Munoz, Restructuring Coordinator, Frank Paul School; Jenne Herrick, Bilingual Education Director, Alisal Union School District; Victoria Bernhardt, Executive Director, Education for the Future Initiative; Mid-California Science Improvement Program (MCSIP) Coaches and Mentors ©1994

BRAIN COMPATIBLE EDUCATION RUBRIC

LEVEL TWO

Physical & Social Values of Environment

- Responsibility to authority is the most important value.
- Classroom has calming colors, music, plants, and potpourri.
- Students sit in clusters with individual access to work tools.
- Yearlong theme and life skills are posted.

Curriculum

- Teacher provides for real-life experiences.
- The curriculum content is aligned with district guidelines.
- Teacher designs a yearlong theme, key points, and inquiries for classroom use which integrate the three areas of science for at least one component of the theme.
- Teacher includes math and science skills essential to the teaching of at least the one component.
- Teacher models and teaches the absence of threat elements as part of the curriculum life skills, lifelong guidelines, decision making, triune brain, multiple intelligences, written procedures and directions.
- Teacher meets with a professional or peer coach who supports the implementation of ITI in the classroom.

Instructional Strategies

- Teacher implements a theme-based brain compatible program for at least five hours a week.
- Teacher predominately uses real-life, immersion, hands-on experiences.
- Teacher implements collaborative learning strategies.
- Teacher uses varied instructional strategies such as agendas, direct instruction, mind mapping, discovery process, etc.
- Adequate time is allowed to let students complete their work.
- Limited choices are introduced through inquiries, supplies, time, doing now or doing it later.

Assessment

- Post-lesson processing about academic or collaborative experiences.
- Use of selected inquiries to assess mastery of key points in such forms as projects, presentations, and some traditional tests.
- Teacher selects work for portfolio folder.

Outcomes

- Students respond positively to enriched environment by participating in all classroom activities, when there is trust and absence of threat.
- Students are actively participating in the classroom by not being absent, being on time, staying on task, actively listening, responding to teachers' questions, engaging in collaborative interactions, and making connections between the classroom and real life.
- Students do not put others down.
- Students' behavior is absent of threat.

BRAIN COMPATIBLE EDUCATION RUBRIC

LEVEL THREE

Physical & Social Values of Environment

- Students are beginning to take responsibility for own behavior through the use of the life skills.
- Classroom has calming colors, music, plants, and potpourri.
- The calmness of the teacher's voice contributes to a settled classroom environment.
- Students are beginning to work in cooperative clusters with individual access to work tools.
- Yearlong theme and life skills are posted.

Curriculum

- Teacher refines the theme and adds at least one additional content area, key points, and inquiries for at least two components of the theme for the year.
- Teacher includes supporting math and language skills which are necessary to the teaching of science.
- Fifty percent of science curriculum is planned and implemented.
- Absence of threat elements are refined and reinforced.
- Teacher will be supported with implementation by working with a peer or professional coach.

Instructional Strategies

- Teacher implements ITI for at least ten hours a week.
- Teacher uses "being there" experiences to make learning real for students.
- Teacher engages students in solving problems in a cooperative manner.
- Teacher consistently allows choices for students through presentations—discoveries, explorations, key points, and inquiries based on knowledge of the theory of multiple intelligence and Bloom's Taxonomy.

Assessment

- Post-lesson about academic or collaborative experiences.
- Use of selected inquiries to assess mastery of key points in such forms as projects, presentations, and some traditional tests.
- Student/teacher selects work for showcase portfolio.
- Assessment of social skills as referred to under absence of threat.

Outcomes

- Students are self-directed during ITI implementation.
- Students are able to solve problems in a collaborative way.
- Students can make connections between what is learned in science and at least one content area to real life.
- Students master and apply social skills in school and outside of the classroom.
- Students begin to demonstrate the use of life skills.

BRAIN COMPATIBLE EDUCATION RUBRIC

LEVEL FOUR

Physical & Social Values of Environment

- Self-responsibility and self-initiated engagement are the most important values.
- Classroom has calming colors, music, plants, and potpourri.
- The calmness of the teacher's voice contributes to a settled classroom environment.
- Students are working in cooperative clusters with individual access to work tools
- Yearlong theme and life skills are posted.

Curriculum

- Teacher refines the yearlong theme and integrates all three areas of science and at least two other content areas, key points, and inquiries for at least 50% of the curriculum for the year.
- Curriculum is based predominately on visible locations which provide "being there" experiences and connections with the real world.
- Curriculum is designed to enhance pattern-seeking and program building.
- The three sciences are integrated for at least 75% of the time.
- Curriculum for collaborative assignments is specifically designed for group work.

Instructional Strategies

- Teacher implements integrated thematic instruction for at least ten to fifteen hours a week.
- Teacher utilizes explorations and discoveries to make learning real for students.
- Students make choices about how they master the key points; including assisting in the development of inquiries.
- Learning experiences are predominately based on real life immersion and hands on of real things.
- Collaboration is regularly used whenever it would enhance pattern seeking and program building.
- Teacher introduces peer and cross-age tutoring to students.
- Teacher introduces the idea of outcomes to students.

Assessment

- Implementing culminating performances chosen by the teacher that demonstrate mastery and application of key points.
- Students can judge their performance through academic and social skills.
- Students select work for showcase portfolio.
- Student/parent/teacher conferences led by the student.

Outcomes

- Students take control of their learning and act in a self-directed manner for the entire day.
- Students demonstrate more shared leadership while doing collaborative activities.
- Peer and cross-age tutoring is being explored.
- Students can make connections between what is learned in science and at least two other content areas to real life.
- Students participate in the design and evaluation of outcomes.
- Students demonstrate life skills throughout the day.

BRAIN COMPATIBLE EDUCATION RUBRIC

LEVEL FIVE*

Physical & Social Values of Environment

- The sense of responsibility for others and the feeling of the community are the most important values.
- Classroom has calming colors, music, plants, and potpourri.
- The calmness of the teacher's voice contributes to a settled classroom environment.
- Students are working in cooperative clusters with individual access to work tools.
- Yearlong theme is evident throughout classroom environment and life skills are an integral part of the class.

Curriculum

- Teacher develops and implements a yearlong theme which integrates the three science areas, all content areas, key points, and inquiries for the entire year.
- 100% of science curriculum is planned.

Instructional Strategies

- Teacher implements integrated thematic instruction all day, all year.
- Collaborative groupings for students.
- Students make choices about the inquiries they do.
- Students help in the selection of key points and take part in writing inquiries.

Assessment

- Culminating performances chosen by the student that demonstrate mastery and application of key points.
- Performance task assesses original, creative, and problem-solving thinking.
- Students/peers self-assessment.
- Students select best work for showcase portfolio.
- Ongoing student/teacher assessment conferences with the use of rubrics.
- Student/teacher/parent interaction and conferences about portfolio.

Outcomes

- Students participate in the design and evaluation of outcomes.
- Students take control of their learning and act in a self-directed manner for the entire day.
- Students demonstrate more shared leadership while doing collaborative activities.
- Students participate in peer and cross-age tutoring.
- Students can connect what they are learning in school to real life.
- Students can creatively solve real-life problems through interrelating and connecting what they have learned in various subject areas and the real world.
- Students use life skills as the basis for interacting with others.

(*Level Five was developed for older learners.)

RESOURCES

The size of this book is not saying that data analysis has gotten easier or that the work is less. This little data analysis book, *Data, Data Everywhere,* is a summary of what we have learned through working with many schools, school districts, states, provinces, and countries.

To see the work in full, you need the following books and websites:

For the fuller version of this data analysis book:

▼ Bernhardt, V.L. (2004). *Data Analysis for Continuous School Improvement.* Second Edition. Larchmont, NY: Eye on Education, Inc.

To see how to set up a database or data warehouse, as well as what analyses and reports are needed to understand how to improve teaching and learning:

▼ Bernhardt, V.L. (2007). *Translating Data into Information to Improve Teaching and Learning.* Larchmont, NY: Eye on Education, Inc.

To see what it would look like if a school or school district did all the data analysis work described in this book. A CD accompanies each book to help schools do this work themselves.

▼ Bernhardt, V.L. (2003). *Using Data to Improve Student Learning in Elementary Schools.* Larchmont, NY: Eye on Education, Inc.

▼ Bernhardt, V.L. (2004). *Using Data to Improve Student Learning in Middle Schools.* Larchmont, NY: Eye on Education, Inc.

▼ Bernhardt, V.L. (2004). *Using Data to Improve Student Learning in High Schools.* Larchmont, NY: Eye on Education, Inc.

▼ Bernhardt, V.L. (2005). *Using Data to Improve Student Learning in School Districts.* Larchmont, NY: Eye on Education, Inc.

To help schools develop, administer, analyze, and use questionnaires.

▼ Bernhardt, V.L. and Geise, B.J. (2009). *Questionnaires Demystified: Using Perceptions Data for Continuous Improvement.* Larchmont, NY: Eye on Education, Inc.

▼ *Education for the Future* Questionnaire Services and Download Center. http://eff.csuchico.edu

For the creation of a School Portfolio.

▼ Bernhardt, V.L. (1999). *The School Portfolio: A Comprehensive Framework for School Improvement.* Second Edition. Larchmont, NY: Eye on Education, Inc.

▼ Bernhardt, V.L. (2002). *The School Portfolio Toolkit: A Planning, Implementation, and Evaluation Guide for Continuous School Improvement.* Larchmont, NY: Eye on Education, Inc.

▼ Bernhardt, V.L.; von Blanckensee, L.; Lauck, M.; Rebello, F.; Bonilla, G.; and Tribbey, M. (2000). *The Example School Portfolio, A Companion to The School Portfolio: A Comprehensive Framework for School Improvement.* Larchmont, NY: Eye on Education, Inc.

We are pleased to announce that the newest version of *The School Portfolio Toolkit* will soon be available online. It is very different from what we are used to with publications. Once you import your data, this website will automatically create your data profile, and prompt you to follow the necessary steps to create your continuous improvement plan and portfolio. Check the *Education for the Future* website (*https:eff.csuchico.edu*) to get the link to the automated *SchoolPortfolio.*

INDEX